THE

SHORTHAND WRITER

THE

SHORTHAND WRITER:

A COMPLETE GUIDE

TO THE

COMMERCIAL, PROFESSIONAL, AND OTHER USES OF SHORTHAND.

BY

THOMAS ALLEN REED

GYAN

Published by

GYAN

Gyan Publishing House
5, Ansari Road
Daryaganj, New Delhi-110002
Phone: 011-47034999, 9811692060
E-mail: books@gyanbooks.com

Distribution Network
gyanbooks.com
India, USA, Canada, UK, Australia

ISBN: 978-93-6208-873-4 (PB)
First Published, 1892

2nd Impression 2024

Printed at: Gyan Press, Delhi.

THE SHORTHAND WRITER
Author: THOMAS ALLEN REED

THE SHORTHAND WRITER:

A COMPLETE GUIDE

TO THE

COMMERCIAL, PROFESSIONAL, AND OTHER USES OF SHORTHAND.

BY

THOMAS ALLEN REED,

Author of "Leaves from the Note-Book of T. A. Reed," "French Phonography," "Two Trips to India;" Officier d'Académie (France), Etc.

LONDON:
ISAAC PITMAN & SONS, 1 AMEN CORNER, E.C.
BATH: PHONETIC INSTITUTE.
NEW YORK: 3 EAST FOURTEENTH STREET.

1892.

PREFACE.

HALF-A-CENTURY'S study and practice of the art of Shorthand as a reporter, professional shorthand writer, teacher, lecturer, and examiner, ought to have given me, if it has not, some qualification for assuming the office of a guide to others who are entering upon the fields of labor in which I have been so long engaged. In a more or less fragmentary way, I have, almost from the commencement of my career to the present time, contributed to the literature of shorthand both as an art and as a profession; and now as the career is, in the nature of things, drawing to its close, I desire to take a more comprehensive view than I have hitherto done, of the many uses to which shorthand has, in these days, come to be applied, and to give my readers the benefit, so far as it can be communicated by the printed page, of whatever experience I have acquired in the various departments of stenographic work. It is a satisfaction to me to know that my other books on the same subject have met with acceptance and kindly recognition from shorthand students and practitioners; and I venture to hope that the following pages, in which I have endeavored to sum up, as it were, the experiences of a lifetime, may not be without their value, especially to those who are entering upon their novitiate. It is for such, mainly, that I have written. The majority of my professional brethren will, perhaps, find little to learn in this volume; the younger ones among them, at any rate, may gather a few hints that will prove serviceable; while to beginners I can safely promise that, if they will give intelligent heed to my counsel, they will avoid some at least of the errors and pitfalls of inexperience, and gain some help towards the attainment of proficiency, if not of high excellence, in the calling which they have chosen.

T. A. R.

CONTENTS.

CHAPTER I.

SHORTHAND AND ITS USES.

PRACTISED among the ancient Greeks and Romans, in use as late as the tenth century of our era, virtually lost sight of in the Middle Ages, revived in this country in the reign of Elizabeth, and subsequently in France, Germany and other continental nations, the art of Shorthand has of recent years undergone a development not only in its methods, but in the practical uses to which it is applied, out of all proportion to that witnessed by any previous generation. No longer an "art and mystery," enshrined in rare and costly tomes, no longer the possession of a few professional or amateur specialists, it has become the common property of the multitude. Chiefly through the labors of Mr Pitman in Great Britain and America, Gabelsberger in Germany, and Duployé in France, to meet the increasing demands of modern life for the curtailment of the time spent in the mechanical work of writing, Shorthand has now been placed within the reach of the humblest clerk of a mercantile office; while as an instrument for the higher uses of the professional shorthand writer and reporter, it has been elaborated and perfected to an extent that seems to leave but little room for further improvement. It has thus opened out a wide field of industry hitherto uncultivated, and, indeed, almost unknown, and, as a consequence, has rendered material aid in the solution of the problem that has perplexed and is still perplexing *pater familias* in all countries—"What to do with our boys?"

It is the object of the present work to set forth the chief uses of Shorthand (to the practice of which the author's life has been devoted) to the student, the clerk or amanuensis, the newspaper reporter, and the professional shorthand writer; to give counsel as to the method to be selected, the modes of study and practice to be adopted and the qualifications, mental and physical, needed to attain success in the various departments of labor which the art has brought into existence.

Of the value of the art itself to the individual and the community it is unnecessary to speak at length. It is now acknowledged on all hands. Shorthand schools are being established in every large town; societies are springing up throughout the land for the cultivation and promulgation of the art; Universities, colleges and public and private schools are giving it a place in their curricula; it is becoming a recognised subject of examination by the large examining bodies of the country; and the increasing number of shorthand candidates that present themselves from year to year testifies to the growing demand for skilled stenographic practitioners. There is hardly a legal or mercantile office of any importance in our large cities in which shorthand amanuenses are not employed to do the clerical work which formerly proved so heavy a burden to the principals or heads of departments, whose time is now available for less mechanical duties. Authors and editors have discovered that by the use of Shorthand they can relieve themselves of much of the drudgery of writing, and that with the removal of the impediment which the use of longhand commonly presents to a rapid flow of thought, there comes a greater facility of composition, as the natural result of a readier mode of expression. Members of Parliament burdened with an extensive correspondence are no longer terrified at the prospect of replying to all their constituents who may address them: a shorthand secretary takes down the needful instructions as rapidly as they can be dictated, and the conscientious Senator can devote the hours that would be otherwise spent in writing, to his Committees and his blue books.

There is, indeed, scarcely any kind of labor into which writing largely enters that may not profit by the use of Shorthand. To the student it is invaluable as a means of taking notes of lectures, making extracts, and writing original compositions. To the barrister or attorney it offers an admirable method of jotting down evidence as it comes from the witness, instead of contenting himself with a mere summary, that may miss the very words on which the point at issue may ultimately turn. To the general reader, who would like to make an occasional record of what he reads, but is deterred by the toil involved in the effort; to the man of business who, remembering that *litera scripta manet*, prefers written memoranda to any recollections of his own; to the traveler who would willingly preserve a diary of his movements, and a record of the sights he has seen and the things he has heard, but shrinks from the wearisome task of committing it all to paper; to the clergyman who would be only too glad to be saved some of the labor involved in the writing of his weekly sermons;—in short, to every one who has much writing to do and desires to minimize the manual effort which it imposes, Shorthand comes as "a boon and a blessing to men," for which, if they avail themselves of it, they will never cease to be grateful. To the professional reporter it is, of course, indispensable. It is part of his stock-in-trade, and its acquisition is a necessary preliminary to the fulfilment of his daily duties. He was at one time, and that within my own recollection, almost the only person of whom this could be said, and was regarded as the envied possessor of an art known only to a favored few, and far beyond the reach of common men. Now, as I have said, it is becoming a subject of every-day education. The demand for its use is daily increasing, and already complaints are being heard that the supply is more than overtaking it. But the field is constantly widening, and there is very little fear of its being permanently overstocked with laborers.

I am not, however, insensible to the dangers and inconveniences arising from a sudden rush of young men and women desirous of employment, to this department of labour. Among those attracted to it are persons who are ill-qualified to enter upon its duties. They spend a few shillings in the purchase of a Shorthand treatise, and perhaps a few pounds in going through a course of instruction at a school, or with a private teacher; and then, without further preparation, consider themselves qualified to undertake the office of shorthand clerk or amanuensis, or even to enter upon some higher branches of professional reporting. They may be indifferently educated, and perhaps lacking in intelligence, but, nevertheless, they expect to succeed in an employment where both education and general quickness of parts are essential to even a moderate degree of success. It cannot be too early or too often stated that Shorthand, without a fairly good education, is of very little value to its possessor. It may be made, as will be shown hereafter, a useful aid to study, a means of education that can hardly be too highly prized; but where it is pursued simply for its own sake, while the cultivation of the intellectual faculties generally is neglected, it will prove a poor instrument at best, and though it may bring the practitioner some amount of employment in the inferior departments of shorthand work, it will never enable him to rise to the higher ranks of the profession.

It is with a view mainly of assisting those who may desire to enter upon the study and practice of Shorthand as a means of livelihood that this book is written. And I desire in the very first chapter to lay it down as an axiom, which admits of no dispute, that if success is to be attained, not only must the art itself be studied intelligently and diligently, but the same intelligence and diligence must be devoted to other subjects; that the general field of knowledge should be as widely cultivated as possible; that no opportunity should be lost of adding to the stores of information already possessed. I shall have occasion to refer to this subject more in detail in dealing with the different classes of Shorthand employment, but I place it in the forefront of this work in the hope that no reader will ever lose sight of it. I have no desire to discourage any who may think of making an occupation of Shorthand, but unless they are willing to enter upon it in the spirit I have indicated, it is only kindness to tell them at the outset that they will do much better to turn their energies into other channels where a studious turn of mind is less essential to success. To many this seems too obvious to require anything more than a passing reference; but long experience has taught me the necessity of enforcing the lesson, especially on young beginners. As an old shorthand teacher, a professional shorthand writer and reporter for many years, and a public shorthand examiner, I have over and over again witnessed the most lamentable failures on the part of young aspirants to Shorthand employment, even in its lower departments, arising mainly, if not entirely, from the want of a good general education. It is perfectly true that I have known excellent reporters and shorthand amanuenses who have had very little early educational training, but they have had exceptionally good natural abilities, and have done their best, by subsequent study, to make up for early deficiencies. I would not say a word to discourage any such students: I would rather do my best to lend them a helping hand; and these pages, I trust, may be of some assistance to them in their efforts. I simply want gently but firmly to warn off all who have no love of books and no desire for mental cultivation, with the assurance that they will never rise beyond the lower rounds of the Shorthand ladder.

CHAPTER II.

History.

THIS book is not intended to be a history of Shorthand, but it would hardly be complete without a few words as to the origin and subsequent development of the art. Like the origin of ordinary writing, the invention of stenographic symbols is involved in some obscurity. The earliest use of shorthand characters is commonly attributed to Tiro, a liberated slave of Cicero, to whose list of Shorthand signs Seneca is said to have made a very large addition. Others have given the Greeks the credit of the invention; and, because it is said that Xenophon took down "in notes" the sayings of Socrates, have arrived at, as it seems to me, the rather rash conclusion that he wrote in Shorthand. It is also stated that Ennius, probably a Greek, when at Rome, 150 B.C., drew up a list of 1,100 Shorthand abbreviations for common use; but the statement wants confirmation. Others, again, like M. Guénin, have carried back the origination of the art to a still earlier period, and from some real or supposed similarity of the Roman *notæ* to the demotic writing of the Egyptians have concluded that the origin of the art, like the origin of modern alphabets, is to be attributed to the descendants of the Pharaohs.

It is unnecessary to enter into a discussion of this rather complicated subject. It is certain that Shorthand was largely used among the Romans from an early period down to as late as the tenth century. The art is referred to by many ancient writers, and some of the Latin poets have fully availed themselves of the license accorded to their craft in their eulogiums on the marvelous feats performed by the Roman *notarii*, or stenographers, who were said to be able to outstrip in speed not only verbal utterance, but thought itself. It is scarcely necessary to say that this is a mere flight of the imagination. The characters that have come down to us clearly indicate a very rudimentary state of the art; and this is further evident from the fact that the Orations of Cato and Cæsar on the subject of the Catiline Conspiracy were taken down in Shorthand by several reporters, each of whom, according to a plan devised by Cicero, wrote a few words, beginning at a pre-arranged signal, and was followed by the others in rotation until his turn came round again. That even these reports, taken with so much elaboration, were not verbatim, may be gathered from the circumstance that Sallust, in recording them in his History, says, "Cæsar, when it came to his turn, spoke *some such words as these;*" and Cato being asked his opinion, "delivered an oration *something like the following.*" But Shorthand was not only used for the purpose of reporting speeches. Several of the Emperors practised the art, and wrote their memoranda and instructions in abbreviated characters, perhaps as much to secure secrecy as to save time. Even the Shorthand clerk, thought to be a product of modern days, was not unknown in the Roman Empire. Pliny the Younger, speaking of his uncle, the great naturalist, says that he was in the habit of sitting with his books at his side, his tablets, and his stenographer. The discourses of some of the early Fathers were recorded by means of Shorthand, and one of them, Gregory of Nazianzen, in his last words, unlike some preachers of modern days, expressed his gratitude to those who had thus preserved his public utterances for the benefit of the Church at large.

The practice of Shorthand, however, was not always encouraged by those in authority. Not being as legible as the common writing, it was regarded as an unsafe method of preserving important documents, and its use for this purpose was sometimes forbidden. Justinian, for example, expressly forbade the writing of his Codex "in catches and short cut riddles of signs." A curious story is told of a Shorthand writer who reported the trial of a centurion for refusing to become a soldier on his conversion to Christianity. Being displeased with the sentence of death passed on the prisoner, the reporter flung his tablets at the head of the presiding magistrate, who straightway inflicted upon him a similar penalty, the appointed executioners being his own pupils, who were to use their iron styluses in carrying out the decree. Many specimens of the Tironian notes have been preserved. They appear to be a mixture of alphabetic syllabic and ideographic symbols. The forms of some of the letters are apparently abbreviations of the corresponding letters in the Greek or Roman alphabet. They have a clumsy appearance, and, as compared with modern stenography, seem ill adapted for easy and rapid writing. Single letters are employed to represent entire words, and all long words are greatly curtailed, only a few of the principal sounds being indicated.

Very little use seems to have been made of shorthand after the tenth century, until the revival of learning throughout Europe. The Romans made no attempt to introduce it into this country; at any rate no traces of it have been discovered. It was not until 1558 that the first system of Shorthand,* if it deserves the name, was promulgated in England, and that was not a revival of the ancient Tironian method, but an original presentation. The author was Dr Timothy Bright, a physician practising in the middle of the reign of Elizabeth, to whom the book was dedicated. Only one copy of this work has been preserved, and that is in the Bodleian Library at Oxford. Bright did not profess to write his words alphabetically. He had, indeed, a Shorthand alphabet, but its letters were only used initially. Each letter took certain additions or modifications, and these were arbitrarily employed to represent, together with the initial stem, certain selected words beginning with the letter in question. These long lists of words had to be committed to memory, a feat which no ordinary student would be likely to undertake, or, at any rate, to accomplish. There is no record of any practical use having been made of Bright's system; but it is interesting as the first attempt in England or in Europe to revive the lost or neglected art. The same may be said of another method that succeeded Bright's by only two years, the art of Brachygraphy, by Peter Bales, which was equally cumbrous, crude and difficult of acquisition.

It was in 1602 that the first really alphabetical system of Shorthand was published in this country. It was presented in a little work by John Willis. The eighth edition appeared in 1623.

* Characterie; or the Art of Short, Swift, and Secret Writing, by Character. Printed at London, in 12mo., by J. Wandate, an assign of Timothy Bright, with the privilege of the Queen, forbidding all others to print the same.

Modern Shorthand, indeed, may be said to date from Willis. His system was alphabetical, and to a large extent phonetic, the sound being followed in the representation of words rather than the common spelling. From his time systems have appeared without number, all more or less indebted to Willis for their alphabetic arrangement. The principal of these are Shelton, 1641; Rich, 1654; Mason, 1672 (adopted by Gurney, and published by him, 1750); Weston, 1727; Byrom, 1767; Taylor, 1786; Lewis, 1815; Pitman, 1837. During the half-century following the issue of Mr Pitman's system, the number of shorthand authors exceeds that of the two preceding centuries. Their systems are mostly founded upon the twenty-six letter alphabet, two or three only having a purely phonetic basis.

The commencement of the *professional* use of Shorthand in modern times cannot be given with any exactness. It has been suggested that the first piece of professional reporting in this country was done by no less a person than Bishop Jewel as early as the middle of the 16th century, before the days of Timothy Bright. That Jewel wrote some kind of Shorthand, possibly of his own invention, there seems to be no doubt, Judging from the description given of it in a Latin work, published in 1573 by Lawrence Humphrey, it could hardly have been a mere abbreviated longhand. "He was always," says the writer, "a tachygraphist and a polygraphist, so that he could express many things quickly and neatly; he took down discourses almost to the word" *(ad verbum)*. This author also says that Jewel wrote "in certain new and peculiar small letters, the interpretation of which would require another Jewel or an Œdipus." Among other things reported by Jewel were the lectures of Peter Martyr in 1549, both in England and in Strasburg. He also acted as one of the official "notaries" at the great disputations of Cranmer, Latimer and Ridley in Oxford in 1554 on the Sacraments of the Altar. None of Jewel's notes, however, have come to light, and we have no evidence of the precise nature of the characters he used.

One of the earliest legal *bonâ fide* Shorthand reports to be found in print is that of the trial of the famous Republican agitator, John Lilburn, at the Old Bailey in 1649. It is described in the title page as having been "Exactly pen'd and taken in Shorthand as it was possible to be done in such Croud and Noise, and transcribed with Indifferent and Even hand both in reference to the Court and the Prisoner; that so matter of Fact as it was Declared might truly come to the public view,—by Theodore Varax (Verax). The second edition." The report is given in the first person, and though probably not strictly verbatim, is far too full to have been taken in longhand. Another trial of Lilburn in 1653 was also very fully reported in Shorthand, probably by Jeremiah Rich, the author of "Semigraphy, or Arts Rarity," 1654; but the report seems never to have been published. A brief and imperfect account of the trial is given in a pamphlet in the British Museum, the author of which promises, "by the aid of the notes of several Shorthand writers . . . . a more exact and large narrative."

About this period, the middle of the 17th century, the reports of State Trials will be found to be much more detailed than those of previous years; and to this date the commencement of professional shorthand writing may be reasonably assigned. In the report of the trial of Christopher Love for high treason, which occurred between the two trials of Lilburn, there is a distinct allusion to the Shorthand writer by the Attorney General; and from other sources we learn that the stenographer's name was John Farthing, who wrote and published a system of his own, 1654. A few years later the Popish Plot Trials, following upon the supposed discoveries of Titus Oates, and the two trials of Oates himself for perjury, were published at great length, and must have been very closely stenographed. The brutal remarks of Jeffreys are recorded with much minuteness, and appear to be a faithful reflection of his character. Towards the end of the century Shorthand reporters constantly exercised their functions in the Law Courts. I have an old Black Letter book containing among other reports the case of "Howard *v.* the Duke of Norfolk" (1683), in the course of which the Lord Chancellor is reported to have said—"It was a cause of Moment and Difference of Opinion, and there are so many Shorthand Writers that nothing can pass from us here but it is presently made public." These Shorthand writers were in all probability employed by the newspapers or by publishers who occasionally printed reports of important trials in a separate form. The Shorthand writer proper, that is the stenographer engaged by the litigant parties to take notes on their behalf, and if necessary for the assistance of the Court, was then unknown. It was not until the 18th century that Shorthand writers in this sense were employed to any considerable extent, and even then they were only engaged in cases of great interest and importance. Their names do not often appear; but the trial of Richard Franklin in 1731 at the Court of King's Bench, Westminster, is said to have been "taken down in shorthand and translated into longhand by Mr J. Weston,"—no doubt the well-known Shorthand author.

The earliest official appointment of a Shorthand writer to take notes of legal proceedings was that of Thomas Gurney at the Old Bailey, about the year 1737, or perhaps a little earlier, by the Corporation of the City of London. His reports of the trials were printed in a periodical publication, the *Sessions Papers*, which has lasted to our own day, but is very little known to the general public. Thomas Gurney retained his office for many years, and is said to have had the help of one or more assistants. His successors in the office of Shorthand writers were Joseph Gurney, 1774; E. Hodgson, 1783; M. Sibly, 1793; Marson and Ramsay, 1796; W. Ramsay, 1798; Ramsay and Blanchard, 1802; J. A. Dowling, 1806; H. Buckler, 1817; Barnett and Buckler, 1848.

The professional use of Shorthand in Parliament is comparatively modern. It is only in the present century that reporters have been recognized and accommodated in the two branches of the Legislature. Till late in the last century the publication of the Debates was discouraged and often forbidden. In 1738 the House of Commons solemnly resolved that such publication was a "high indignity"; rigorous orders were often given for the exclusion of strangers, and hence there was very little opportunity for the stenographer to follow his craft in St Stephen's. There are, indeed, very early reports of speeches in both Houses, but these could hardly have been supplied by professional stenographers. It has been frequently said that the debates in Parliament in the reign of Elizabeth were taken in Shorthand by Sir Simon d'Ewes, and afterwards transcribed into longhand. The printed volume containing these reports is in the British Museum, and anyone who will take the trouble to refer to it will see that stenography could not have been needed for its compilation. It is, as the compiler states, a collection from the journals of the House and other sources, and not a transcript of his own notes. It is difficult to say when Shorthand was first used for Parliamentary utterances. The early reports are too brief to admit of the supposition that they were thus recorded. Members themselves sometimes printed their own speeches, or gave their notes to others for publication, and occasionally we find members taking notes of entire debates, transcripts of which have come down to us, and are accepted as authentic records. Even as late as the days of Johnson and Cave, when fuller reports were given, there is but little indication of the employment of Shorthand. The manner in which Johnson wrote his reports has often been told, and need not be here repeated. He used, mainly, materials supplied by others; but we hear little or nothing of professional Shorthand reporters. There are some printed debates in the House of Lords between 1735 and 1743, being the transcript of Shorthand notes taken by Archbishop Secker. These reports, however, are so brief that they might have been easily taken in longhand: and much fuller reports of the same debates are given in the "Parliamentary History," taken from other sources. Again, from 1768 to 1774, a very industrious Member of Parliament, Sir Henry Cavendish, took copious Shorthand notes of the debates in the House of Commons, and the transcript, made partly by himself and partly by a clerk, is now in the British Museum. It extends to 48 volumes, in some of which there are Shorthand notes written in Gurney's system. The reports were apparently intended for publication, but the intention was not carried out. Sir H. Cavendish says: "My original design was to take down the heads only of the several speeches, but finding by practice even my inferior skill adequate to something rather more extensive, in the subsequent Sessions of Parliament the debates will be found more at large and with very few omissions, except in the case of a few members whose rapid delivery outran my ability to keep up with them." He also apologises for other imperfections on the ground of his inconvenient situation at the time of writing, and of the disorder which occasionally prevailed. "And sometimes," he quaintly adds, "those favourite words 'hear,' 'hear,' so frequently echoed through the House forbade all hearing."

In 1802 an Act was passed in reference to Election Committees appointed to hear petitions against the return of Members of Parliament; and amongst the provisions of that Act is one for the appointment by the Clerk of the House of a Shorthand writer, who was to be sworn, to attend such Committees for the purpose of taking notes of the evidence. From that time the Election Committees (till their abolition), Private Bill Committees, and Select Committees of both Houses have been attended by Shorthand writers. The Messrs Gurney obtained the appointment, and their firm continues to this day to supply stenographers to Parliamentary Committees. The admirable manner in which their work has been done is universally acknowledged, and all Shorthand writers may feel proud of their achievements. I have been informed by the Messrs Gurney that their books of daily engagements go back to 1785, just over a century; that they contain entries of law cases taken for solicitors, and that they seem to indicate that the course of business was established as a regular thing at that time. I need not say that no other existing firm of Shorthand writers has so long a history. If we extend it back to the appointment of Thomas Gurney at the Old Bailey, it embraces a period of a century and a half. During the early portion of this time they occasionally published their notes of celebrated trials, especially criminal ones, which were the more highly valued because the newspaper reports of those days were extremely imperfect. They also published some volumes of sermons by Whitefield and other preachers.

It is difficult to say when Shorthand writers were first employed in Courts of Law to take notes of cases, not for publication, but for the parties concerned. The earliest list of Shorthand writers that I can find in the Law List is in 1789, when the following four names appear:—Blanchard William, Dean Street, Fetter Lane, 12; Gurney Joseph, opposite Fetter Lane, Holborn, 128; Hodgson Edmund, White Lion Row, Islington, 13, or at Mr. Walmesley's,

Stationer, Chancery Lane, 3. No doubt Shorthand writers had been regularly employed in Court before this period, although their names do not appear in the earlier issues of the Law List; but I have not been able to trace the time of their introduction. I have heard, indeed, of transcripts of Shorthand notes, similar to those supplied to solicitors at the present day, as early as the middle of the last century, but I have never seen any. I have no doubt that legal Shorthand writers were then employed, but their numbers must have been very small. The law reports, till a comparatively recent period, were prepared independently of Shorthand by barristers who attended the Courts. Some of the official reporters, who are still barristers, now write Shorthand; but in important cases they have recourse to the notes of professional stenographers when they are available. The number of professional Shorthand writers now practising in the London Courts is very large. Those belonging to the Institute of Shorthand Writers number about seventy, and there are others who do not belong to that body.

For sermon reporting, Shorthand writers were very early in the field. Great prominence is given by the authors of all the early systems to the advantages of Shorthand for this purpose, and most of them provide special contractions for frequently recurring texts and pulpit phrases. Those were probably intended, chiefly, for the use of persons taking notes of sermons for their own private use, which has always been a favourite practice among the congregations of popular ministers. But professional note-takers were sometimes employed for the purpose; or took notes and published them on their own account, not always to the satisfaction of the preachers. Thus, in an old volume in the British Museum there is a sermon by the Rev. Nathaniel Hardy as early as 1653, published by the preacher himself, who says in his preface:—"If the fear of an abortive birth by some unskilful notary had not enforced me, it (the sermon) should have been buried in privacy." This pretty clearly shows that the practice of sermon reporting then prevailed; and it has continued ever since. It could often be pursued when other kinds of reporting would be dangerous. When political harangues were forbidden, and might have brought the speakers and publishers to the scaffold, greater latitude was allowed in regard to pulpit utterances; which accordingly presented a wider and safer field for the exercise of the stenographer's craft.

Reference has sometimes been made to the employment of Shorthand Writers in taking down the plays of some of the earlier dramatists, including those of Shakespeare himself. The instances cited by Mr. Levy in his pamphlet on the subject have not satisfied me that the many errors appearing in the early editions of Shakespeare's plays were due to Shorthand. Many of them, I think, were mere misprints, while others might have been the mistakes of actors themselves, who dictated the parts to amanuenses, or perhaps wrote them out from memory. I know that allusions are made to "brachygraphy men" as having been the culprits in some of these cases; and perhaps they may have been at a later period, but not, I think, in Shakespeare's time, when Shorthand was in its infancy.

The more modern professional uses of Shorthand writing will be dealt with in subsequent chapters under their appropriate headings.

CHAPTER III.

Choice of a System.

IT is probable that the majority of those who consult these pages have already made their selection out of the multitudinous systems of Shorthand offered for their acceptance; but to those who have not taken even this initial step a word of counsel may be useful, and, indeed, may naturally be expected. It is difficult to conceive a much more embarrassing task than that of making such a selection without the aid of an expert. Every author naturally proclaims his system as superior to all others, and as combining all the requirements of an English Shorthand. Nothing is easier than to obtain testimonials of approval from persons more or less (generally less) qualified to pronounce an opinion upon the merits of a particular system; and I am sorry to say that nothing is commoner than to read the most mistaken estimates on this head. One is unwilling to attribute them to wilful mis-statement, but the least that can be said of them is that they are too often founded on ignorance and inexperience. It can hardly be expected that the beginner should take the trouble to examine minutely every advertised system of Shorthand, or even every system that has succeeded in finding favour with professional reporters and Shorthand writers; for it is scarcely necessary to say that some of the most belauded methods have not attained this distinction after years of eulogium and advertisement. But even if the task were undertaken it would prove to be one of great difficulty; for until the student has gone so far as to learn at least one system so as to be able to write it with some facility, he is not in a position to judge of the comparative merits of other systems. Most beginners, therefore, will naturally ask for guidance in making their selection. My own answer to the inquiry, "What system shall I choose?" is unhesitatingly "Pitman's." I am far from saying that there are not other systems which have good claims to consideration as having furnished writers who have done excellent work in practical note-taking. Some have the merit of great facility of acquisition; others not so easily acquired are extremely brief; and others, again, while somewhat long and cumbrous, have the merit of being distinct and legible. I know, however, of none which combines the qualities of brevity, legibility, and ease of acquisition to a greater degree than Pitman's Phonography. It has, moreover, the unquestionable advantage of general acceptance. It does nearly the whole of the reporting of the English speaking world. Its text-books are cheap and easily accessible, and it has a literature of its own of great value to its students and practitioners. Its principal journal has a weekly issue of 25,000, and a dozen other Shorthand periodicals written in the same system have a wide and increasing circulation. There are, also, numerous Phonographic Societies throughout the Kingdom, besides a large National Association for promoting the development and culture of the system and the interests of its writers, as well as testing and attesting the qualifications of Shorthand teachers. I do not propose to enter upon any lengthened discussion as to the comparative merits of Phonography and other Shorthand systems, which would require a volume for its adequate treatment. It is sufficient to say that Phonography, by the work it has done and the position it has attained, has proved its excellence to an extent that will certainly justify any intending student in readily accepting it as an instrument which will serve all the purposes to which he will have occasion to apply it.

CHAPTER IV.

How to Learn Shorthand.

ASSUMING that the reader intends to follow my advice, and acquire a knowledge of Pitman's Phonography, if he has not already done so, I may, not unnaturally, be expected to give a word of advice as to the mode of setting about it. The art may be acquired with or without the services of a teacher. The text-books are so complete, and the general literature of the subject is so extensive, that no person of ordinary intelligence and reasonable diligence can experience much difficulty in gaining, not a mere smattering but a full and sufficient knowledge of the principles of the system; and, this once secured, the needed mechanical dexterity is mainly a matter of persistent application. Where a teacher, therefore, is not at hand, the student should not hesitate at once to begin without any such assistance. But if personal instruction is available, recourse should be had to it. Teachers of Phonography are now to be found in every large town and in many of the smaller ones throughout the kingdom; and for a small sum the student may be conducted privately or in class through all the details of the system in such a manner as greatly to facilitate its acquisition. Some teachers offer their services to instruct pupils through the medium of the post; but this is a method that I cannot recommend. An instructor can communicate very little in writing that may not be easily gathered from the books. But there is a decided advantage in having a personal guide who will answer questions and solve difficulties as they arise in the course of study, and guide the student in his daily practice. The pupil, or his friends, should of course be careful to select a competent teacher, one who has not only a perfect book knowledge of the system, but sufficient dexterity in its practical use to be able to follow a slow speaker *verbatim*. A higher degree of speed, indispensable to the professional reporter or Shorthand writer, is not a necessity to a Shorthand teacher. As in the case of music, many men of great manipulative dexterity are incapable of imparting effectually and agreeably to others the information they themselves possess. The art of teaching is *sui generis;* it needs a special instinct and special qualifications, without which no amount of manual skill will avail. And let me say emphatically that no teacher should be chosen who does not possess general intelligence and a fairly good education.

But if the student is compelled for any reason to dispense with professional aid, he should send for the three text-books and make a start without delay. He may, if he chooses, purchase them at once; but, if he prefers it, he may content himself with the "Teacher," a little sixpenny book, which contains all the elements of the system, and which, unless he is in a violent hurry, will provide him with all the material for practice that he is likely to need for a few weeks, or, if he proceeds slowly, a few months. The first thing to be learned is the alphabet of single letters consisting of straight and curved lines in various directions for the consonants, and dots and dashes in three positions for the vowels. These may be committed to memory in a few hours at most, and the student will have but little difficulty in comprehending, by the aid of the illustrations given, how they are grouped together in the formation of simple words.

But though the translation of these elementary exercises may prove an easy task, the writing of the characters with neatness and accuracy will require great care and attention. And here, on the threshold, let me impress upon the student the necessity of great precision. The letters being simple geometrical signs, and depending for their meanings upon their slope, thickness, length and position, if any of these distinctive features are neglected or slurred over, their true significance is necessarily hidden or obscured. If the pupil is accustomed to drawing, he will be able easily to preserve these distinctions; but without some such training more or less difficulty will be experienced in the early days of Shorthand practice. A simple straight vertical stroke (representing the letter *t* in Phonography), easy as it seems, presents an initial difficulty to many a student. He has probably been accustomed all his life to write longhand on the slope from right to left, and in his first efforts to write the Shorthand letters he experiences an almost irresistible tendency to write all the upright characters in that direction; and sometimes in the effort to correct this tendency he actually falls into the habit of sloping them the other way. The curved letters, too, segments of the circle, present difficulties of their own. To strike a curve in the proper direction with accuracy and freedom does not come by nature: the hand must be trained to these exercises, and the earlier the training begins the better. All the Shorthand characters, therefore, should at first be carefully *drawn*, without the least attempt at rapidity of movement. They will probably, in most cases, appear stiff, and sometimes even shaky, indicating laborious effort on the part of the writer; but if the proper configuration is preserved these early defects are comparatively unimportant, and will gradually disappear. But if the learner begins with a scribble, and is inattentive to the precise outlines to be traced, he will acquire a habit which may be fatal to his future success. Exactitude is of the essence of Shorthand writing, and should be sedulously cultivated at the outset. Let the pupil, for example, when he has written say a line of *f's*, observe to how many of them he has failed to give the proper slope, so that they may be easily read for the upright *th*, and he will have a good illustration of the dangers which beset the careless writer. Of all the curves, *m* and *n* are perhaps the easiest to trace: most of the others present some little difficulty to the untrained hand, and should therefore be made the subject of special practice until the writer finds that he can strike them with accuracy and without undue effort.

Another stumbling-block often encountered in the early stages of the student's progress is the proper junction of the consonants. If they are carelessly joined, their distinctive character is lost, and they may be misread for single letters. Some of the curved consonants are connected without an angle, and flow into one another with graceful ease, as ;
and, always assuming that the proper slope is preserved, there is no danger of misreading. But straight consonants cannot be united without an angle, and if this mode of union is

not distinctly shown, the letters cannot be deciphered with any degree of certainty, Where the angle is acute, as the writer can hardly fail to indicate it; but in the case of a right angle, and still more an obtuse angle, unless great care is taken he will probably miss the angle altogether, so that *tk* will be written closely resembling the letter *f*, and will be written which may easily be misread for the letter *r*. But perhaps the greatest care is needed in the junction of a straight letter and a curve without an angle, as *pn*, *mp*, *nr*, *rm*. The learner, and even the advanced student, when writing these forms at all rapidly, will in all probability give them the shape of large curves in which there is no indication whatever of a straight letter. To begin quickly with a perfectly straight line, and then suddenly to change the course, without a perceptible angle, and trace a curve, or *vice versâ*, with strict accuracy, is no easy matter, requiring, as it does, a delicacy and precision which a heavy hand is not likely to attain: and if it is found unattainable I should recommend the student, in the few cases in which such joinings occur, to pause an instant at the junction, and, for the sake of clearness, make an angle with the succeeding letter. I have sometimes recommended learners to practice this kind of junction by writing over and over again a simple sentence presenting several illustrations of it, as, for example—

Get me a penny map of Stepney.

The rapid and accurate writing of such a sentence I regard as a phonographic *tour de force*; and it may serve the purpose at once of a training exercise for the young student and a scriptorial gymnastic for the amusement of the more advanced. A test of accuracy may be found in a dotted line at the point of junction, thus which will clearly show whether the curved letter and the straight letter have been distinctly written, and kept from merging into each other.

The right use of the vowels occasionally presents some little difficulty to the beginner. It is here that the phonetic character of the system, and its divergence from the common spelling, are chiefly displayed. That *ā* and *t* do not spell *at*, or *ē*, *t*, *et*, and that the short vowels in these syllables have really no relation to *ā* and *ē*, but are the short sounds of *ah* and *ā* respectively, and have therefore to be paired with them, is a revelation to many a student, and, for the first week or two of his practice, he will be very likely to misapply these symbols both in reading and writing. And so with the other pairs. A little attention, however, will soon familiarize him with their proper use. He will learn to see that the letters are grouped, not in the promiscuous fashion of the common alphabet, but in accordance with their mutual relations. Many learners do not think it necessary to trouble themselves with the scientific analysis of English spoken sounds which forms the basis of the alphabet. Nor perhaps is it needed for practical every day purposes. But an intelligent pupil should assuredly not wholly ignore the theoretical principles that underlie the system which he has adopted. Every teacher, whether in public or in private, should make them a part of his curriculum. If a knowledge of these principles do not greatly assist the learner in the mechanical part of his practice, it will at least give him an increased pleasure in his work. It is sometimes made a matter of reproach to the Shorthand writer that he is a mere mechanical drudge. Let him not afford any pretext for the calumny by neglecting at the very commencement of his efforts to study the elementary principles which form the very foundation of the method he is practising. And if in addition to a general knowledge of the phonetic analysis of his own language he endeavors to acquire some familiarity with the construction of the organs of speech, with the laws of the production of sounds, and especially of spoken sounds, he will not only be enlarging the domain of his studies in cognate subjects, but will come to feel an interest in phonetic Shorthand quite apart from its advantages as a lightener of the labor of writing, and as a money-earning instrument.

The compound consonants will offer no serious difficulty to the learner; but the double vowels of the *w* and *y* series, long and short, are sometimes the source of a little perplexity.

They should be carefully memorised and their use be clearly understood. I have heard many professional reporters speak of them with as much disrespect as Sidney Smith's friend did of the Equator, and make it a boast that they never observed the distinctions between the different vowels of the series, content only to mark the initial *w* and *y*, and allowing the succeeding vowel to take care of itself. I cannot commend this lordly indifference, which may lead to error when least suspected. The student, at any rate, will do well to make himself master of these as of all the other details presented in the "Teacher" before proceeding to the next text-book. No advantage will be secured by hurrying over the ground with undue haste. The pupil should feel his way as he goes, making sure of one step before taking another.

The "Teacher" mastered, the work of a few weeks, according to the ability and diligence of the student, he should lay it entirely aside and adopt the "Manual" (price 1s. 6d.) as his guide. He need not at this stage trouble himself about the question of speed. If he can write his shorthand as rapidly as he can longhand this is all that he requires for the first two or three months. Speed can only be attained by writing from dictation, and this, in the "Teacher" stage, is quite needless, simple copying and writing exercises in the ordinary way sufficing for all practical purposes. "More haste the less speed" has perhaps no more appropriate application than in the case of a Shorthand student who seeks to acquire a fluent style before he has laid a good foundation of theoretical knowledge.

The "Manual" opens out a wider field than the student has hitherto cultivated. There are but few new characters introduced, and not many additional principles of contraction; but there is a longer list of "grammalogues," letters representing entire words, which have to be committed to memory, and there are numerous rules for the formation of words—that is, for the selection of outlines for the many words whose consonants may be written in more than one way. It is here, perhaps, that the learner most needs the guidance of an expert, whether in the form of a book or a personal teacher. In consequence of the numerous double and treble consonants in the system, it is possible to write most words of more than one syllable in several different ways. This may be considered a disadvantage and a source of difficulty and confusion. In reality it is an advantage. Not only do these compound letters provide extremely brief modes of expressing clusters of consonants that, if written singly, would occupy considerable space and require proportionate time to trace, but, as the learner will soon discover, they afford a convenient method of distinguishing words containing the same consonants without the necessity of inserting vowels, thus increasing the legibility while preserving the brevity of the writing—a happy combination of excellencies which, apart from its phonetic basis, places Pitman's Shorthand at the fore-front of stenographic systems. The "Manual" may require another month or two to assimilate; and when the process is complete the student may reasonably consider the question of speed, which I have advised him to disregard at an earlier stage. By the time he has mastered the system as propounded, that is, when he finds that the forms come readily to his mind and that he can write them without hesitation, he should have no difficulty in writing 60 or 70 words a minute, and a quick learner will greatly exceed this rate. His first efforts at contraction will naturally be in the direction of omitting the vowels. But this should be done very gradually and cautiously. Practice alone, both in reading and writing, will guide him in this respect. He will not be long in discovering that the longer the word the less it will need the insertion of vowels. Very few words of more than two syllables require any vowel whatever, that is, where the rules for constructing the consonant outlines are observed and the words are kept in their proper position. Short words, especially monosyllables, and words with a single consonant and several vowels, as *iota*, *Anna*, cannot dispense with one or more of their vowels. As a rule, if a short word begins with a vowel it should be written in preference to any other vowel that the word may contain. Both initial and final vowels are usually more suggestive, and therefore more useful, than intermediate ones. On no consideration should the student begin the habit of omitting vowels until he is perfectly familiar with the proper method of inserting them. Nor should he be in a hurry to devise special contractions of his own. They may at first seem very convenient and unobjectionable; but the probability is, that as he proceeds he will find it advisable, if not absolutely necessary, to discard them. It is much better, adopting the principle of *experto crede*, to follow the lines laid down in the instruction books than to diverge into untrodden paths—that is, until the writer has, by considerable study and experience, entitled himself to assume the rôle of an explorer and a guide.

When a speed of 80 words a minute has been acquired, the learner may take the last step in his elementary career and study the pages of the "Reporter." But here again a word of counsel and caution may be given. Nothing is more deceptive than tests of speed as they are sometimes applied. A student will ask a friend to read to him, an easy passage containing short and frequently recurring words, for one or two minutes; and if, by a supreme effort, he manages to get down the passage at the rate of 100 words a minute, and read it immediately afterwards without making many mistakes, he straightway concludes that that is his normal rate of speed, and congratulates himself accordingly. In order to verify his conclusion, let him take another passage of a different character, say a leader in the *Times*, or a page of history, containing a fair admixture of long and short, familiar and unfamiliar words; let him further extend the period of his test to five or ten minutes; and, still further, let him put his writing aside for a week, that he may receive little or no assistance from his memory, and he will be surprised at the difference in the result. If he has written at the same rate he will find a great part of his writing undecipherable; or if he has limited his speed in accordance with his ability to write legibly, he will probably find that it has not exceeded 70 or at most 80 words a minute. Tests of speed, to be at all trustworthy, should be made with ordinary prose matter, not too difficult and not too easy. It should not contain too many proper names, or recondite allusions, or involved sentences, all of which may perplex and hinder the writer either in his notes or in his transcript. But of this I may have something further to say later on.

If, on these lines, the learner finds that he can write without much strain, 80 words a minute, and *read them easily*, he may, as I have said, proceed to the "Reporter," where he will find further lists of abbreviations and rules for applying them. He can, if he likes, commit them all to memory in the ordinary way, or he may prefer to memorize a few at a time, and trust to his daily reading and writing practice for acquiring a complete knowledge of them all. The printed Shorthand exercises should be carefully copied several times until they can be read with ease without the aid of the longhand key. The key itself should then be rendered into Shorthand without reference to the printed exercise, with which it should afterwards be compared with a view to the detection of errors. Every departure from the original need not necessarily be regarded as a mistake. It may be only a permissible alternative form; but it will be as well to note it, and follow forms of the text, for which there may be good reasons, not perhaps obvious to the student.

One feature in which a certain amount of divergence will be almost inevitable is the extent to which words are joined without lifting the pen. Everything, it has been said in regard to other rules, depends upon the application, and it certainly is so with reference to the phonographic principle known as "phraseography." Hard and fast rules cannot well be laid down, and much must be left to the discretion of the writer. No two writers, however orthodox and uniform their outlines may be in other respects, will exhibit the same similarity in their phraseographic junctions. It may be safely said, however, that the best writers are not those who are most given to this species of abbreviation. It is rather the young tyro who delights in long and laboured phraseograms, and is jubilant over combinations fearfully and wonderfully constructed, which would fill a practised scribe with supreme contempt and unutterable horror. I think the extreme practical phraseographic limit is reached in Mr Pitman's published exercises, the "Phonographic Phrase Book" (1*s.*), containing above two thousand useful phrases, and that the pupil should rather endeavor to keep within than go beyond it. Some hints on this subject will be found in an article on phraseography in "Leaves from the Note-book of T. A. Reed" (vol. 2, p. 115). It will be sufficient here to say that the main essentials of a good phraseogram are the following:—

1. It should be clear, distinct, legible, and not likely to clash with single words or other phrases.
2. It should rarely exceed five or six words.
3. None of its characters should ascend or descend so far as to interfere with the writing in the line above or below.
4. Its junctions should be easy, natural, unforced, such as the hand can readily form without halting or hesitation.
5. It should not include any difficult or unfamiliar word.
6. The words should be grammatically or naturally connected, and such as would be read without a pause, and would not require to be divided by any mark of punctuation.

If any one of these canons (so to designate them) be violated the phraseogram *pro tanto* stands condemned. The least important perhaps is No. 3, at any rate in regard to the objection to a descending outline, since when the writer comes to it in the next line he can easily "skip" an inch and avoid a collision. But an invasion of the occupied territory of the upper line may lead to confusion, and should certainly be avoided.

I have assumed, in most of the advice given in the foregoing pages, that the student has been practising without the aid of a teacher. He may be reminded, however, that there is one kind of personal and gratuitous assistance of which he may well avail himself. I refer to the Phonetic Society. The members of this Society (whose names are published from week to week in the *Phonetic Journal)* undertake to correct the exercises of learners through the post. I have already expressed the opinion that postal tuition is not of any great value in comparison with oral instruction; but at the earlier stages of his practice a learner may find it an advantage to write an occasional exercise of a page or two for correction by some phonographer who, by his membership of the Society, volunteers his services for the purpose. A passage may be copied from a newspaper, every other line being left blank to receive the examiner's correction: the newspaper cuttings should be enclosed together with the exercise. This kind of assistance may be useful to a beginner, and even at a later stage, but unless the gratuitous instructor is known to be himself an advanced student and practitioner, it will hardly be safe to *assume* that he will prove an efficient and trustworthy guide throughout.

Where two young phonographers can pursue their studies together they will find a decided advantage in this method. There is nothing in which combined study and practice will be found more beneficial than in the case of Shorthand. When they are sufficiently advanced to be able to write freely from dictation, the students can write and dictate in turns; and, as they proceed, discuss outlines, rules of writing and the like to their mutual advantage. Nothing can be pleasanter than when two or more members of a family thus unite their efforts in a common study, each acting in his turn as dictator (not, it is to be hoped, in the offensive sense of the term), and all doing their best to add to the general stock of knowledge. If, moreover, instructive and suitable books are selected for the regular writing practice, a double object may be secured, and a foundation laid for a love of literature, which will prove a priceless possession in after life. A good historical volume, say one of Macaulay or Froude, which combines the charm of style with interesting historical information, will be found very serviceable for the purpose. The object should be to choose a book in which all can feel an interest. A scientific work bristling with technical terms would be most unsuitable; unless, indeed, it dealt with a subject which the learners were studying or desired to study; and in that case the selection would, of course, be a judicious one. I should hardly recommend a light novel, with a good deal of dialogue, since both the narrative and the dialogue are apt to drag and lose all their vivacity when solemnly read at the rate of 80 or 90 words a minute. Poetry again, especially blank verse, is not to be recommended as a writing exercise. It is troublesome enough to the professional reporter, who may spend hours in poring over a passage which he has taken down accurately, but which he does not know how to display in the proper lines; and it will be still more difficult to the Shorthand student.

If there happens to be a Shorthand Society in the town where the student resides he will do well to join it, if only for the sake of the "speed practice" which such societies commonly afford to their members. Meetings are arranged, at which some member, or a person engaged for the purpose, dictates at varying rates of speed to those assembled. And here I may be permitted to interpolate a word as to the importance of having a good reader for practice of this description; one who can not only regulate his pace at the required speeds, but can enunciate distinctly, and read intelligently and agreeably. A jerky, indistinct, or unpleasant delivery is very unsatisfactory, and will repel rather than attract the students. A judicious reader will do his best, first to make himself well heard, and, when he comes to words of more than ordinary difficulty (of which he can only judge if he is himself a Phonographer) will slightly slacken his pace for a second or two, making up for lost ground by a corresponding acceleration at a convenient moment when some easy passage presents itself.

With regard to actual note-taking, I mean taking down the words of a public speaker, the student will naturally ask for some advice as to when and how far he should seek for practice in this direction. I recommend him to defer this practice until he can write from dictation about 80 words a minute. Most speakers speak at a far higher speed than this, and I do not consider it desirable that the learner should attempt to take down speeches greatly exceeding the rate of speed that he has attained. The most that he will do in such cases is to take down a few disjointed phrases, which will give little or no idea of the general purport of the entire address. He may hardly, indeed, secure an entire sentence, but leave off in the middle and "take up the running" at some convenient or inconvenient point in a subsequent sentence; the general result being a chaotic mass of verbiage, as devoid of meaning as a piece of printer's "pie."* This is at once unsatisfactory and discouraging. Above everything the pupil should avoid writing nonsense. If he cannot keep up with the speaker he is following, he should at least see that what he does write is intelligible as far as it goes, and endeavour to get down the substance, if not all the words, of the speech he is reporting. This will be almost impossible with a slow writer following a rapid speaker. His great effort will probably be to get down as many words as he can, and his attention being concentrated on this object, he will have none

* A technical term for lines of type that have been upset, and re-set for distribution, the letters having become hopelessly disarranged.

left to devote to the still more important consideration of securing the sense of the words to which he is listening. It is only when the task of writing becomes easier, requiring less conscious mental effort, that the mind is free to apply itself to the work of sifting and selecting from the words that fall upon his ear those which, since he cannot catch them all, are most suitable to be transferred to his note-book. For these reasons I advise my young friends not to be in haste to practise on public speakers, but to wait until they have attained something like the speed I have mentioned, and then to begin, if possible, with as slow a speaker as they can find. Nor must they be unduly discouraged if their first efforts at actual note-taking are utter failures. The beginner is apt to be disconcerted when he finds himself practising his art, as it were, in public. He innocently imagines that every eye is upon him, and feels ill at ease as he struggles on in the vain endeavour to keep pace with the speaker. He is perfectly conscious that he is making wholesale omissions, and has a lurking suspicion that other people know it too. Altogether he passes a *mauvais quart d'heure*, and begins to think of giving up in depair. But he need not abandon his task. His experience is a familiar one, and he will learn to smile at it himself as he feels his way, and is no longer disturbed by the thought of neighboring inquisitive eyes.

In taking notes of a speech the reporter is generally a few words behind the speaker. He may at times be ten or a dozen words in arrear, but he should endeavour to keep within three or four words if possible. In the latter case a sudden increase in speed will not disconcert him ; but it may be fatal if he is already a long way behind. It is quite possible to be too close to the speaker. Singular mistakes may arise from the proximity. Thus, I have myself written the figures "40" as the beginning of the word "fortitude." They were, of course, written before the final syllable "tude" had been uttered, or had time to reach the brain. In the same way, when close upon the speaker's heels, I have written the grammalogue for "very," and have had to cross it out on discovering that the word was "verified," which required an entirely different commencement. In such cases the writing and the utterance must have been practically simultaneous.

I have recommended the student to follow carefully, as far as possible, the *sense* of what he is writing. I know it has often been suggested that the reporter who is busy with his pen in recording a speech, and is perhaps straining every nerve to keep pace with the speaker, has no brain power left to take in the sense of the words, for seeing the point of an argument, or apprehending the general structure of a discourse. There is very little truth in this suggestion; in many respects it is the very opposite of true. I do not deny that an unskilled Shorthand writer, who has not the forms at his fingers' ends, ready to be traced without the slightest hesitation, who has consciously to *think* of the outlines he is drawing, may find it difficult, if not impossible, to follow his speaker in a double sense, in thought as well as in word. Nor will I go so far as to say that even an accomplished reporter, whose Shorthand forms are his obedient and agile slaves, may not now and then find himself in the same position. When hard pressed by a fluent speaker, discoursing, say, on a technical or unfamiliar subject, it is quite conceivable that even he, with all his skill and experience, may be so much occupied with the effort to secure an accurate record of the words as to be unable to follow with anything like ease or comfort the train of thought or the narration of facts with which he has to deal. But under ordinary circumstances an efficient stenographer finds that his practice of note-taking not only is no obstacle to his mental apprehension of the spoken words, but in some cases absolutely assists him to grasp their meaning. He is compelled to listen with great care, to concentrate his attention upon the words and sentences as they fall from the speaker's lips, and not allow himself to be diverted from his task; his ear is a cultivated one through his habit of note-taking, and, in spite of the disadvantage of not being able to look at the speaker, he catches many words that would escape a casual listener; and if he knows that he has to give, not perhaps a verbatim, but a condensed account of what is said, he has the strongest reason for endeavouring to seize the points as they arise. The practice of note-taking, therefore, is a help, and not a hindrance. Of course, I know that it is possible for the Shorthand writer, especially when he has an easy speaker to follow, to pursue his work in a mechanical sort of way without having the remotest idea of the words he is writing. He may be even pursuing a totally independent train of thought, planning his holiday tour, wondering how the tailor's bill is to be paid, recalling the incidents of last night's pantomime, and knowing no more of what he is recording than his pen or his note-book. But this is not a habit to be encouraged. The trained and conscientious reporter, as a rule, follows the sense as well as the sound; if not, he pays the penalty of falling into many a pitfall. Ludicrous mishearings are often the result of inattention to the sense of spoken words; and, unless the mistake is detected in transcribing—an operation that is also sometimes conducted without due deliberation—it may get into print, very much to the confusion of the reporter and the annoyance of the speaker.

But it is not always that a reporter, however carefully he may be attending to the sense of a speech, is successful in his effort to catch it. The mishearing of a single word may entirely mislead him. This is an accident that can never be wholly avoided. The reporter may be perfectly sure that he has not heard the right word; it may be the veriest nonsense; but he has no time to stop and consider. His best plan in such a case is to write down exactly what he has heard or thought he has heard, however absurd it may seem; and when he comes to transcribe, the proper words, which are probably somewhat similar in sound, may suggest themselves to him. If, owing to the apparent absurdity of the words, he omits them altogether, he will have nothing but the context to enable him to arrive at a solution of his difficulty.

CHAPTER V.

EXAMINATIONS AND CERTIFICATES.

IF the student desires to have his efficiency tested and attested, there are several examinations open to him, in connection with which Certificates are granted to the successful candidates. There is, for example, Mr. Pitman's "Speed Certificate" examination, which is open to all Phonographers. These examinations are held at various centres recognized by Mr. Pitman. The candidates are tested at various speeds of dictation, their transcripts, when made, are duly examined, and if they are deemed satisfactory, containing not more than two per cent. of errors, certificates are given for the speed attained.

There is also the examination of the Society of Arts, to which many hundreds of candidates annually resort. It is held usually in the month of April, in connection with the other examinations of that Society, at its various centres throughout the United Kingdom. A small fee (2s. 6d.) is paid by each candidate to defray the necessary expenses. The writers of any system are admitted, but the candidates are recommended by the Society to adopt Phonography. Efforts have been made to induce the Society to withdraw this recommendation, but they have not been successful. The test is entirely by means of dictated passages. Three passages are set by the examiner, to be read in seven minutes, at 80, 110, and 140 words per minute respectively. The candidates may transcribe any or all of these passages. A satisfactory transcript of the first passage secures a third-class Certificate; of the second, a second-class; and of the third, a first-class; in addition to which medals are given to the best of the first-class candidates. The papers, when completed, are sent to the Society in London, and then forwarded to the examiner for his award.

There are Shorthand examinations, too, in connection with

the Oxford and Cambridge Local Examinations; but as these are chiefly for boys and girls at school they are more elementary in their character, and no great speed is required. For the "Commercial Certificate," however, recently established by the University authorities, a Shorthand "pass" requires a speed of 70 words a minute for a period of five minutes, while a speed of 100 words per minute for the same period is awarded a pass "with distinction." The examinations for this certificate are held at various centres, and have been established by the Oxford and Cambridge Schools Examination Board for the benefit of the elder boys when leaving school, to whom the certificates may be of great use in obtaining good situations in mercantile offices. Shorthand is but one of the subjects prescribed, and is optional on the part of the candidates. Any system may be written, as in the Oxford and Cambridge Local, but, as a matter of fact, nearly all the students who present themselves are writers of Phonography. The examinations are held in the summer.

The recently formed National Phonographic Society is another Shorthand examining body, but its examinations are chiefly for teachers' diplomas. They are far stricter than any others that have been instituted, and demand not only a reasonable speed on the part of the candidate (80 words a minute being the minimum), but a thorough acquaintance with all the principles and details of Phonography, and the ability to impart the knowledge to others. The Society also holds speed tests for its own Fellows, but accepts as a qualification for Fellowship the Certificates of the Society of Arts (first-class), and of Mr. Pitman (120 words per minute). Membership of the Society only requires a knowledge of Phonography, no special rate of speed being required.

If the student desires to present himself for any of these examinations, he should not omit the necessary preparatory training. Very many candidates attend them who are utterly unprepared, and therefore fail to pass even in the lowest grade. Knowing the kind of test to which they will be subjected, they should get a friend to read to them at the prescribed speeds, and for the time required, and then carefully transcribe their notes, religiously marking every error, however slight, writing neatly and legibly, and not overlooking the punctuation, the absence of which will tend to disqualify the candidate. And not until the task can be accomplished with tolerable ease and certainty should the student send in his name for an examination. Nor should uneducated pupils be recommended by their teachers to seek these certificates. The want of education will be sure to reveal itself in the transcript, not only in the failure to catch words a little out of the ordinary run, but in mis-spellings, the want of punctuation, and an inability to construct sentences properly—defects that no examiner can overlook. In order to form some idea of the kind of passages prescribed, the candidates should refer to those of previous years if they are available. Those of the Society of Arts can always be obtained; the examination programme for the year always containing reprints of the papers set in each subject in the preceding year. The passage set for the third-class certificate is generally of a simple, easy character; but those for the higher certificates are somewhat more difficult.

CHAPTER VI.

Commercial Shorthand Work.

THE most extensive use of Shorthand in the present day is its application to what may be called commercial purposes. In almost every large business office a large portion of the clerical work is performed by Shorthand writers. I now use the term not in the restricted and professional sense in which it will be employed in the later pages of this work, but in the wider and more usual acceptation of the term, as signifying a Shorthand clerk or amanuensis. I begin with this description of work because it is the lowest round of the ladder of Shorthand employment, and is the department to which the majority of Shorthand students propose, at first at any rate, to devote themselves. It presents a vast and varied field of labor from that of the junior clerk who has just left school and is able to take down at a moderate rate (80 or 90 words a minute) the corresponence of his employer and transcribe it into a good clear longhand, to the senior clerk whose notes are perhaps transcribed by others, and who occasionally undertakes far more difficult work than mere writing from dictation, often jotting down brief memoranda rapidly suggested rather than dictated by his principal, to be subsequently expanded into a long letter or an important document. Between these there are many intermediate stages, and the remuneration varies very much according to the value of the services rendered. The youth who is making his first start may have to content himself with a salary of ten or fifteen shillings a week. If he is wise he will not be at first as solicitous about the amount of his earnings as about the nature of the opening which presents itself, and the opportunities which it affords of subsequent advancement. This, in a good office, will come in due course if it is deserved; and it will depend not merely on the stenographic ability displayed by the writer, but on his general intelligence and assiduity. The complaint often made by employers of labor of this kind is that the young Shorthand clerk is a mere office machine, writing down the words dictated in a purely mechanical manner, often transcribing them without an effort to comprehend their purport, and thus inevitably falling into the most ludicrous errors. It is true that such complaints are sometimes made in a querulous spirit, and by persons who expect highly skilled labor for less remuneration than is commonly given to the lowest manual employment. But they are not wholly imaginary. So far as they are well grounded, they usually arise from the circumstance that so many young men—I am afraid I must also say young women—are ready to offer their services as Shorthand clerks and amanuenses without possessing the necessary mental equipment for the employment they seek, and hardly even the manipulative dexterity which, necessary as it is for their work, they have foolishly regarded as the chief, if not the only requisite qualification for its performance. Ignorant of the elementary principles of grammar, without an inkling of the rules of punctuation, ill informed on general topics, making no effort at mental culture, and perhaps even writing an indifferent longhand, they scramble through the Shorthand text-books, and imagine that they may successfully undertake the office of a Shorthand clerk, or even aspire to a reportership on a country newspaper. I am far from wishing to over-state the case in speaking of the importance and the necessity of a good education to a Shorthand writer, even in this preliminary stage of his development. It is sometimes absurdly exaggerated. From the description given of the needed qualifications, a person of ordinary endowments and fair commercial education might not unnaturally shrink from a task which would seem to call for at least a University education and the possession of intellectual faculties of the highest order. "*Quod est absurdum.*" All that is required in this respect, certainly for an ordinary Shorthand clerk in a merchant's or a solicitor's office, is a fair education such as is now open to every youth in the land, moderately good abilities, and the power of writing good grammatical English. It is necessary to insist upon this. Many employers are indifferent grammarians, and if the clerk, in transcribing his notes, fails to correct grammatical slips, or is unable to give an intelligible rendering to a confused mass of verbiage which has been dictated to him, he will not be likely to meet with speedy promotion. If the young Phonographer aspires, as I hope every one of my readers does, to achieve distinction, and advance to higher posts, something more even than this will be required. Besides increasing his Shorthand speed, for which his daily practice may suffice, he should take every opportunity of adding to his stock of general knowledge, cultivating the love of reading, not simply the daily newspaper, good, of course, in its way, but the best literature of his country. The knowledge of another language than his own will greatly assist in his mental culture, and may now and then prove extremely serviceable in his daily employment. For commercial purposes, French, German and Spanish are the most useful. The student, unless he has exceptional linguistic abilities and ample leisure, can hardly be expected to master all these; but he might at least attempt one, and it will be far better to learn this thoroughly than to acquire a smattering of two or three. French is, on the whole, the most generally serviceable, and unless there is any special reason, as there may well be, for learning one of the other languages, it may be confidently recommended. If this recommendation is followed, I hope I shall not be suspected of interested motives in referring the reader to a little work of my own, "French Phonography,"* in which he will find a number of useful grammalogues, contractions, &c., and hints as to the best method of expressing French words generally. The adaptation is not intended for Frenchmen themselves, who will naturally prefer systems of their own, but for English students of Phonography who desire to utilize the Shorthand knowledge they have already acquired, and save themselves the trouble of compiling lists of abbreviations of frequently recurring French words and phrases. For it is almost needless to say that, without some such assistance, the taking down of a foreign language from dictation would be impossible.

The Shorthand clerk, moreover, should endeavour to make himself familiar with the general routine of office work, the keeping of accounts, and the like, so as to make himself a

* "French Phonography," an adaptation of Pitman's Phonography to the writing of French, by T. A. Reed, price 1s. (Isaac Pitman and Sons.)

"good all-round man," who may be relied on, in emergencies, to render effective help beyond the immediate sphere of his own department. The technical details of the business carried on in the establishment in which he is engaged should be diligently studied. It is here that beginners sometimes experience difficulties that at first seem insuperable. He may have to take down matter that is wholly unfamiliar to him, full of technical expressions which he hears for the first time; and if the dictator is at all rapid, or not very distinct, the poor dictatee has a hard time of it, and is sorely tempted to relinquish his employment. If he has been a studious youth, and fond of reading, technical expressions will not have the same terror for him. He may not improbably have met with them before; or, if not, his general knowledge will easily enable him to turn to the necessary sources of information for the assistance he requires. In many instances the clerk, if he is alive to his opportunities, and not preternaturally dull, will pick up the terminology of the establishment as he goes along. But he should not be content with this. He should make it a point to study some useful work, say of an elementary character, which will not only bring before him the unfamiliar words that he will have to record, but give him such an outline of the general subject as will enable him to understand the meanings of the particular words in question as well as the general bearing and significance of the dictated matter in which they occur. How essential this is to really successful and satisfactory work every thoroughly experienced Shorthand practitioner can testify. Without such a qualification the position of a Shorthand amanuensis may sometimes be humiliating in the extreme. Take the case of a young man who has accepted an engagement in the office of an electrical engineer, and who opens his note-book for the first time for the purpose of taking down from his principal a letter or other document for transcription into longhand. Principals are not always considerate. They are apt to think that a Shorthand clerk should have an intuitive familiarity with every department of human knowledge, and do not make allowances for youthful inexperience, to say nothing of nervousness and dread of failure. The "chief" then rattles out—for perhaps he is in a hurry or naturally impetuous—a string of sentences about "ohms," and "volts," and "farads," and "ampères," and "commutators," and "electrolysis," till the luckless scribe is in a whirl of excitement, bordering on frenzy. He cannot summon up courage to stop his dictator, but struggles on in abject misery, and leaves off in a bath of perspiration. He looks at his employer in mute despair. The latter simply says, "Copy as soon as possible; post goes out in half an hour." Half an hour! Half a year would not suffice to give a proper translation of those bewildering sentences, which are as meaningless to the writer as an Accadian inscription. An hour's glance at a shilling text-book would have saved him half his agony and all his humiliation.

Legal technicalities are not quite so formidable as scientific terminology; but they are numerous, and often prove puzzling to the young Shorthand clerk. As this is a department of Shorthand work employing a large number of hands, and in which many students are every day seeking employment, there is really no excuse for their not doing their best to qualify themselves for the posts to which they aspire, not merely by their dexterity as penmen, but by their intelligent comprehension of what they are employed to write. It is commonly believed that the ordinary law writer, who spends his days and often his nights in copying legal documents, never bestows a thought on the meaning of what he writes. Such a reproach should never attach to the Shorthand writer, in whatever grade, who, for his own reputation and for the credit of his calling, should do his best to lift it far above the dead level of mechanical drudgery, to which inconsiderate persons sometimes assign it.

Railway offices afford another extensive field for the labors of the Shorthand clerk. Here the technicalities are not far beyond the range of ordinary everyday language; but they include many words and phrases, not difficult in themselves, but of such frequent occurrence as to render it extremely desirable to provide for them a brief and easy mode of expression: the names, for example, of the principal railway companies in the kingdom, and the common phrases used in correspondence between one office and another as to the details of the traffic and the general working of the line.

In regard to legal and railway work, the student may consult with advantage the pages of the "Legal Phrase Book"* and the "Railway Phrase Book,"† which contain extensive lists of abbreviations for commonly occurring words and phrases in these departments, from which he may make such a selection as may best suit his purpose, without undertaking the needless task of committing them all to memory. To provide complete lists of special contractions for every description of Shorthand work for which the Shorthand clerk may be engaged would require an amount of space and labor not at my command; and no Shorthand writer, however wide and varied his practice, could possibly need them. My own little work, "Technical Reporting,"‡ which is primarily intended for professional Shorthand writers and reporters, may prove serviceable to the Shorthand clerk who is or expects to be employed in taking down matter of a scientific character, containing, as it does, copious, though by no means exhaustive, lists of classified abbreviations suitable for law, medicine, physiology, mechanics, &c., together with general hints as to the formation of similar contractions on the same or other subjects on similar lines. Phonography, by the admirable use it makes of every kind of practicable stenographic material easily lends itself to the provision of these special abbreviations. Where no other convenient outline seems to suggest itself for a common word or phrase greatly needing it, the principle of intersection may be resorted to, and with its aid, in addition to all the other ingenious contrivances with which the system abounds, it is rarely that a flowing, expeditious and legible form cannot be devised by the practitioner himself. Where such contractions have been provided for him he may as well avail himself of them as give himself the trouble to invent and test abbreviations of his own.

The salaries of Shorthand clerks in commercial and legal offices vary greatly according to the qualifications required. They may be said to range from a pound or thirty shillings a week to three or four pounds, the last mentioned sum being rarely exceeded.

* "Phonographic Legal Phrase Book," an adaptation of Phonography to the requirements of legal business and correspondence. 6d.

† "Phonographic Railway Phrase Book," an adaptation of Phonography to the requirements of railway business and correspondence. 6d.

‡ "Technical Reporting," comprising phonographic abbreviations for words and phrases commonly met with in reporting legal, scientific, and other technical subjects. 1s. 6d.

CHAPTER VII.

SECRETARIAL AND DICTATION WORK.

IN addition to the employment of Shorthand in connection with office work, which I have called "Commercial Shorthand," there is a wide field for its employment for secretarial purposes. Not only Members of Parliament, who have to keep up an extensive correspondence with their constituents, but literary men, editors, managers of large business concerns, noblemen and many others who can afford the luxury, are in the habit of engaging private secretaries to relieve them of the drudgery of clerical work, to keep their papers and books in order, and to fulfil a number of other duties commonly associated with the secretarial office. It is impossible to give a list of these. There is no general rule respecting them. They vary with every appointment, and are a matter of special arrangement between the parties concerned. One secretary may have nothing to do from morning to night but to write incessantly from dictation and transcribe his notes into longhand, nothing being left to his own origination or discretion; while another may have a wide range of duties of a more or less confidential character—interviewing visitors, writing letters (not necessarily from dictation), making purchases, keeping accounts, looking up authorities, making extracts, in fact assisting his employer in all save menial capacities, and being treated more as a trusted friend and counsellor than as a paid servant. Between these extremes there are of course numerous gradations. I have known the case of a private secretary one of whose duties has been to keep the private visiting list of his employer's wife, and even (will it be believed?) her betting book! The position therefore is sometimes a delicate one, needing great tact and experience, and involving relations of great trust and confidence. The usual qualifications for the office are a good education, a gentlemanly bearing, general trustworthiness, and a good handwriting. To this is now often added a knowledge of Shorthand. Even if this is not specifically required, it can never fail to be a decided recommendation to an applicant for the vacant post, and it should therefore be cultivated by every one who contemplates employment of this character. But the man who will be most esteemed is one who, in addition to his Shorthand, is able and willing to make himself (to use a term commonly applied to humbler occupations) "generally useful" to his employer, carrying out his instructions, and even anticipating his wishes, with unvarying promptitude, intelligence and fidelity. This, indeed, is the rule of all service.

Besides regular secretarial work such as I have described there is a great deal of *occasional* work in which the services of a fairly skilled Shorthand writer are called into requisition. An author has a number of rough notes and memoranda which he wishes to expand into a volume, and he finds it much easier, with his papers before him, to dictate to an amanuensis employed for the occasion than to prepare his own manuscript for the printers. An official or a scientific expert has to draw up a long report of an inquiry that he has been making, and, time being an object, he engages a Shorthand writer for a few days or weeks in order to facilitate its preparation. I have often known lecturers prepare their lectures, and preachers their sermons in the same way; and many a political speech before being delivered to the public has been rehearsed and dictated to a Shorthand writer, afterwards to be amended, expanded, or curtailed, as may seem desirable. The translation of plays and other works is often expedited in the same manner. These are but a few of the many occasional uses to which Shorthand is applied, quite apart from its regular professional employment. It is true that professional Shorthand writers and reporters are sometimes employed to undertake work of this character; but, unless it is unusually difficult, it may reasonably be undertaken by a well-informed young man or woman in his or her early days of Shorthand practice, always supposing that a speed of 100 or 120 words a minute, estimated in the way I have described, has been attained. A Shorthand clerk who leaves his office at five or six o'clock may sometimes find employment of this nature for a few hours in the evening. These long hours might be too much for a continuance, but an occasional spell of hard work for a few weeks, or even months, will not be beyond the powers of one who is blessed with a good constitution, whose habits are temperate, and who has learned how to get through his work easily. The last mentioned qualification is perhaps largely a matter of temperament; but, like every other faculty, it can be cultivated. Fussiness in work of all kinds leads to more wear and tear, mental and bodily, than more prolonged toil without worry or excitement.

I ought not to omit one special department of dictation work that is highly suitable to the class of Shorthand writers to which this section of my work is devoted. I refer to that obtainable in the offices of professional Shorthand writers, especially those who practise in the London Law Courts. Each firm of Shorthand writers of any standing has a staff of assistants employed in taking notes of cases in Court, or transcribing the notes of their principals, or (as is most common) taking them down from dictation and then transcribing what they have written. But when there is any great pressure of work, such as a busy season often brings with it, extraneous aid is called in, which is often rendered by Shorthand clerks who are engaged during the day and are glad to supplement their income by employment in the evening, or by others who happen to be out of employment, and can thus devote the whole of their time in meeting the emergency that has arisen. The ordinary course of proceeding is this: When a Shorthand writer returns from the Court after a "turn," long or short, of note-taking, he finds several assistants, permanent or occasional, awaiting his arrival. He then dictates to the first, say for ten minutes or a quarter of an hour, then to the second, third, and perhaps a fourth and a fifth. By this time the first will have made his transcript, and is ready for another "take," and so with number two and the rest in due succession. In this way the transcript, as it is called—not the "report"—is practically being prepared as quickly as the Shorthand writer can read his notes and get them taken down, the only delay being in the transcription of the last series of "takes," but this interval is usually occupied in the examination, and, if necessary, the correction of the manuscript by the dictator. In some instances the Shorthand writer does not dictate his own notes, but delegates the work to one of his assistants who has been trained for the purpose, and is familiar with his handwriting. The advantage of this method is, that the Shorthand writer can tear a few pages from his book in Court and send them away for transcription, while he continues his note-taking; so that when he comes to his office at the end of a long turn, perhaps extending over the entire day, he finds a big batch of manuscript ready for his examination. Both methods have their advantages and disadvantages, which it is unnecessary to discuss here. In this kind of dictation work the assistant is naturally most valued whose manuscript is most accurate and legible. Nothing is more annoying and irritating to a Shorthand writer with perhaps a hundred pages of manuscript before him than to be frequently stopped in his reading to correct some careless blunder on the part of the dictatee; and great is the relief which he feels when, after wading through a "take" full of these provoking inaccuracies, he comes upon the work of an assistant of whose habitual correctness he has had long experience. In the latter case, unless some special difficulties present themselves, he will, if pressed for time, simply glance at the pages as he turns them over, and be content to let them go without a more minute inspection. Highly appreciated also in these cases is a good clear longhand, which is considered more creditable to the office, and is certainly much more easy to examine. A speed of 120 words a minute is commonly sufficient for this class of work, but the assistant who can, when required, write at a more rapid rate, and transcribe accurately and rapidly, will, other things being equal, always be preferred by the busy Shorthand writer, who is anxious to turn out his transcript in the shortest possible time. I may mention that the rate of payment for this kind of casual work is 2d. per "folio" of 72 words. At a busy time a fairly skilful dictatee, if kept well occupied, should have no difficulty in earning from £1 to £2 a week or more in his evening hours. There is, however, some uncertainty in work of this description. A case which is expected to last many days or weeks may suddenly break down, and the expectations built upon the prospect of its continuance are rudely shattered. One qualification of a good dictatee I had almost forgotten. He should not be in a hurry to leave before the evening's work is finished. A Shorthand writer is sometimes left at eleven o'clock at night with insufficient help to finish his concluding pages because one or two of his transcribers have found it necessary to leave him "to catch their last train." The man who has no last train to catch, or who will rather miss it than put his employer to inconvenience, will be the one most valued when it comes to be a question of selection.

It is hardly necessary to explain that Shorthand work of the kind I have been describing in the last few pages is only to be found in London and in a very few of the large cities in the kingdom where important legal proceedings are carried on requiring the services of professional Shorthand writers. Newspaper reporters do not often dictate their notes to assistants, but transcribe them with their own hands. In a few cases, however, casual help from outsiders—Shorthand clerks and others—is called in by them, and paid for at the usual rate. But unless the assistant is a rapid as well as an accurate transcriber, very little time is saved by his employment.

CHAPTER VIII.

NEWSPAPER REPORTING.

ONE of the most important, if not the most extensive, uses to which Shorthand is applied in this country is its application to the purposes of newspaper reporting. A considerable proportion of the space of almost every newspaper, both metropolitan and provincial, is now occupied by reports of public addresses of every kind, political, social, scientific, religious, and what not; including, of course, the proceedings of the principal legal tribunals of the country; and for the production of most of these reports Shorthand is an indispensable instrument. In America full reports of public speeches in the newspapers are almost unknown, and hence Shorthand is by no means an invariable qualification for a newspaper reporter, whose greatest recommendation is that he should be a "smart" news collector and paragraphist. In England, so much importance is attributed to the utterances of leading public men that a reporter, except for certain special classes of work that will hereafter be referred to, who is not a skilled Shorthand writer stands very little chance of profitable and regular employment. In my early days a good deal of newspaper reporting was done by means of abbreviated longhand. Even in the "Reporters' Gallery" men with good memories and other mental endowments were able to dispense with Shorthand, and present very fair, though not *verbatim* reports of the speeches delivered in both Houses of Parliament. Lord Campbell, who, when a young man, was a Parliamentary reporter on the staff of the *Morning Chronicle*, distinctly tells us that he never learned to write Shorthand, and rather takes credit to himself for his ignorance of the art, and for his reporting achievements without any such mechanical aid. But in his time the public requirements were very modest in comparison with the demands of to-day, when every subscriber to a penny paper expects to see on his breakfast table or in his morning train full reports, not only of what passes in the Legislature, but of all important addresses delivered the day before in the most distant parts of the empire. To satisfy this imperious demand, an army of Shorthand writers is busily engaged every hour of every day in taking and transcribing notes for the wire and the press.

But let no Shorthand student imagine that any amount of stenographic skill will, of itself, secure him an appointment as a newspaper reporter. He may go gaily into training for speed, achieve his 200 words a minute, and triumphantly flourish his certificate in the face of the newpaper editor or proprietor; but unless he is able to back up his application by a still more substantial proof of general intelligence and education his prospect will be a poor one, and he will be nowhere in the race with a man of higher intellectual capacity but inferior Shorthand attainments. What I have said on this subject in regard to the Shorthand clerk is still more applicable to the reporter. In the case of the clerk everything he does is usually under the direct supervision of his principal, and much of his work consists in taking notes from dictation, which he can transcribe, in many cases, precisely as they appear in his notebook, with very little exercise of his own discretion. The reporter, even when a junior, ordinarily works on a wholly different platform. His powers of composition are always called into play, not merely in the construction of paragraphs of news, but in transcribing his Shorthand notes of speeches. He is required from the first to exercise his judgment as to what should be retained, omitted, condensed, or amended. There is no slavish transcription in any department of his work. It is true that he is subject to a certain amount of supervision on the part of his editor or chief reporter, but it is only a very general oversight, and for much of what he does he has to rely upon his own unaided and uncontrolled discretion. Even at the Police Court, which is often the first scene of his labors, he finds himself in a position of serious responsibility in which an error of judgment may have serious consequences to himself and his paper. He sits in judgment on what cases he shall publish and the extent to which he will report them, and a slight mistake in a statement of fact, or in the name of one of the parties concerned may raise a hornet's nest about him. In condensing an ordinary speech into a half or a quarter of its original length, he is again confronted with the necessity of selection; and if he is unable to grasp the salient points of the address, and present them, not necessarily in the speaker's words, but to some extent in his own, he falls below the standard of the requirements of newspaper reporting. But especially is demand made upon whatever literary ability he possesses when he is called upon to undertake what is known as descriptive reporting. If he is a Shorthand writer, and nothing more, he will be hopelessly at sea when attempting to describe the commonest incidents of the day, to say nothing of an important public ceremony, every detail of which is a matter of public interest and calls for minute, and if possible, graphic description. It is true that when there is a large staff available, this department of reporting is generally allotted to hands specially qualified for it; but on many papers, employing only one, or at most two reporters, such a division of labor is not practicable, and a certain amount of descriptive ability is therefore expected from each member of the limited staff of the establishment. It is obvious, therefore, that a mere knowledge of Shorthand, however essential to a reporter, is but one of several qualifications needed for the satisfactory fulfilment of his duties.

With reference to his acquisition and early practice of Shorthand, I need not repeat the advice which I have given to the Shorthand clerk and amanuensis, which is equally applicable to the reporter. The earlier he begins the better. Few men become really successful practitioners of Shorthand who take it up after twenty-five years of age. In youth the fingers are supple, and adapt themselves to any mechanical exercise better than at a more advanced period of life, when also other interests and occupations are more apt to interfere with systematic and persistent application. Thirteen or fourteen is a good time to begin, but at any time between that age and twenty a youth may, with diligence and fair abilities, reasonably expect to acquire the needed facility of execution. If he has a naturally heavy hand he will require more time and labor than his lighter-fingered brother, and may not be able to indulge in the same refinements of abbreviation, requiring delicate and minute distinctions in outline which are not easily preserved. Lightness of hand, though largely a matter of constitution and temperament, may be cultivated with advantage. Some writers grasp their pen or pencil so tightly that an easy, flowing style is never acquired. This can only be accomplished by a light touch, which also has the advantage of enabling the writer to continue his work for a much longer period and with much less fatigue than would be possible with a heavier hand. This applies both to longhand and shorthand. Where the pen is tightly held, a couple of hours' continuous writing is felt to be a toil; producing, in the case of rapid note-taking, a sense of considerable fatigue. But a reporter who holds his pen lightly, and is perfectly familiar with his Shorthand, will write either longhand or shorthand for half a day or more without any such laborious exertion or sense of weariness. I have myself taken Shorthand notes for ten hours continuously, with an interval of only a few minutes, filling more than two hundred closely written pages, each containing about five "folios," and could have gone on, without much difficulty, for an hour or two longer. I take no credit to myself for this. Having naturally a light touch, I have simply tried to cultivate it, as many others have done with the same result. The only pressure on the pencil or the penholder which is needed is just enough to give the fingers a perfect command over it, so that the forms may be traced firmly and clearly, but not stiffly. Any pressure short of this will lead to a careless, *degagé* style of writing, which the writer himself will not find it easy to decipher. A happy and judicious combination of firmness and lightness is the goal at which every young Shorthand writer should direct his efforts.

The practical duties of a newspaper reporter are, as I have already said, very various. In some cases, they consist largely of reporting meetings, lectures and public addresses of every kind; in others this is but a subordinate part of the reporter's duty. In London and some of the larger towns there are many reporters who are almost exclusively thus employed; but in the provinces generally the daily routine of a reporter's life is of a much more varied character. It forms, however, in the great majority of cases, so conspicuous a part of his labors that I do not hesitate to place it first in the list.

The fulness, again, with which speeches are reported is also a matter of the greatest possible variety, presenting every gradation between a brief summary of a few lines suitable for a Reuter's despatch and a verbatim report extending over many columns. Some papers devote themselves to special subjects, and give full reports of everything pertaining to them. The ordinary newspaper is contented with more or less condensed reports of meetings and speeches of a routine character, but when an eminent statesman or other distinguished personage speaks in the district which it covers, or an important trial takes place of exceptional local or general interest, the reports, if not verbatim, are usually very extended.

I will deal first with full reports. The arrangements made for these vary according to the staff of the paper and the time of its publication. If it is a daily morning paper, and the meeting takes place in the evening, several hands are required for the purpose of supplying a full report of the speeches, each taking his turn at the work. In order to provide copy quickly for the printers, and to get all the reporters at work as soon as possible, the shorter the "turns" taken the better. By means of five minutes' turns, six or seven hands can keep up with the speeches as they proceed, each reporter writing out his turn (at the reporters' table if necessary, or in a convenient room adjoining) and being ready for the next turn when the time comes round. In this way the entire copy can be in the printers' hands within half an hour of the close of the meeting; or still less if the concluding turns are shortened to two or three minutes. If only two or three hands can be spared for the work, a different arrangement is needed. Longer turns become necessary; but one or two short turns should be taken at the commencement in order that no reporter may be kept idle while he might be at work. If at the close one reporter finds himself with more notes than he can well transcribe in time, he can generally obtain assistance from one or more of his colleagues who have concluded their own labors. If only one reporter is available, a verbatim report for immediate use is of course a matter of impossibility; but if the requisite interval is allowed, as in the case of a paper publishing only once or twice a week, there is no difficulty in the matter.

When a small corps is engaged to take very short turns at a meeting, in order to keep up a continuous supply of copy for the printers, it is as well, where practicable, for one of the staff to take a check-note throughout. This enables him to see that the turns are properly fitted together, to supply any gaps that may have been left between them, to prevent overlappings, and generally to assist in securing accuracy and despatch.

Great care should be taken to prevent the slips of the different turns getting mixed. Where several reporters are engaged the name of the writer should be placed at the commencement of each turn, and also the name of his predecessor, thus, "Davis follows Smith." And at the end of the turn it is as well to write the name of the succeeding reporter, thus, "Jones follows," or capital letters may be used instead of names. Without some such arrangement it is impossible for the printers to keep the copy in order. Batches of manuscript containing the uncompleted slips of several reporters, if not thus distinguished, may easily get into confusion, resulting in delay, and, I am afraid, bad language.

The time occupied in transcribing may be taken roughly at five or six times that occupied in note-taking. A quick writer will transcribe easy matter more rapidly; but it is not safe to arrange for less than this. When the matter is at all difficult, or the speeches are unusually rapid, a still longer time should be allowed. Newspaper columns vary greatly in their capacity according to their length and the kind of type employed. A *Times* column ("minion," the type in which reports are usually printed) contains rather more than 2,000 words, which can be writtten in two hours, or less if there is no difficulty in regard to the notes or other cause of delay in the transcription. Exceptionally quick writers have transcribed a column in little more than an hour; but this is a rate of speed that could not be maintained, and occasional "spurts," either in note-taking or transcribing, should never be taken as criteria of ordinary speed. It is possible to write in longhand sixty words a minute, or more, for a very short period. The utmost that I have been able to accomplish in a single minute is 65 words: these were mostly short ones, and were written not from dictation or from notes, but in the form of an ordinary sentence composed during the act of writing.* Such speeds, however, are beyond the range of practical daily work.

---

* A facsimile of the passage will be found in the *Reporters' Magazine*, Sept., 1885.

The suggestion has often been made that a reporter's Shorthand notes should be handed over, without transcription, to compositors who have been trained to read and compose from them. I fear that this is but an ideal condition of things, and incapable of practical realization. If every speaker were distinct, deliberate and grammatical, needing little or no revision, if every reporter wrote with accuracy and legibility, and if the trained compositor were thoroughly familiar with the Shorthand characters, the achievement would be a matter of no great difficulty, that is, in cases in which very full reports were required. But until the ordinary style of speaking is wholly reformed, and reporters learn to be far more exact in their penmanship than they usually are, it will be simply impossible to dispense with a transcript of the notes or something equivalent to it. The very few cases in which compositors have been known to set up from a reporter's notes* cannot be taken as examples of what may be accomplished in everyday work. It is too much to expect that even a highly skilled phonographic compositor should not only set up types from rapidly written notes, but do all the necessary revision and reconstruction of sentences which forms a large part of a reporter's duty in the work of transcription. A more practical suggestion is, that the transcript itself should be written in a moderately vocalized Shorthand for the compositors. In this there would be but little difficulty, and a good deal of time might thus be saved. The compositors, no doubt, would require extra remuneration, and, indeed, might reasonably expect it.

There is another method for saving time in transcription which I have sometimes adopted with advantage—that of dictating to two longhand writers simultaneously. The ordinary way in which this is done is to dictate from two distinct parts of the notes; but this has the disadvantage of compelling the reader, after dictating a few words from one page, to turn to another and dictate a few words from it, and

---

* One of these was the well-known instance of a report by Mr Isaac Pitman of a speech by Richard Cobden, the notes of which were slightly revised and "vocalized" before being handed to the compositor. Another was a case of my own, as far back as 1847, in which a few pages of a very easy speaker were given untouched to the printer, by whom they were set up with perfect accuracy.

so on throughout. This constant break of continuity is prejudicial to speed, causing frequent stoppages, unless the matter is exceptionally clear and straightforward. My own plan is what I have called the twin-slip method. It is to dictate to two amanuenses, who write on slips of paper ruled exactly alike. When six or seven words have been dictated to one writer he writes them on the first line: then a similar number of words is dictated to number two, who writes them on *his* first line; the reporter then dictates a second line to number one, followed by another to number two; and so on till the two slips are filled. This done, the slips are gummed together at the side (a margin being left for the purpose), so that the lines come in exact apposition, and the writing is read continuously across from one slip to the other. The best way is to have the slips prepared and gummed beforehand, so that by the simple application of moisture they can be joined without difficulty or delay. This method has the advantage of enabling the reporter to dictate to two writers without any break of continuity, which greatly facilitates his labors. In this way he may get through, as I have often done, a newspaper column (or thirty folios) in three-quarters of a hour. Where good Shorthand dictatees are obtainable they are, no doubt, better than two longhand writers; but, as they cannot always be procured, the plan I have mentioned is worth adopting when time is pressing. Of course it is not practicable for official reports, which have to be neatly written and bound up; but for the printing office, where a constant change of writing is immaterial so long as it is legible, the twin-slip system is perfectly feasible.

I can say nothing of the suggested system of the reporter dictating into an Edison's phonograph, the words to be subsequently reproduced by the machine as slowly as required and taken down by a longhand writer for the press. I see no reason why this may not be done if the machine is available; but at present it is not on the English market, and in the absence of any trustworthy evidence as to its capabilities for press work, I am unable to express any definite opinion on the subject.

Although most newspaper reporters are now expected to be able to take a verbatim note when it is needed, it is comparatively rarely that their ability in this respect is put to the test. The bulk of a reporter's work in the way of speech taking is not verbatim but condensed reporting. A meeting lasting a couple of hours, if reported fully, would occupy from six to eight columns of an ordinary daily paper; and two or three such meetings might occupy all the available space, to the exclusion of other and far more important matter. It is, therefore, in the great majority of cases, the duty of the reporter to condense the speeches he reports into a reasonable compass in proportion to their importance, not necessarily from his own point of view, but from that of the newspaper which he represents. And this is one of the most responsible duties which he has to discharge. As to the precise length to which the report of any individual speech or meeting should extend, he may be required to follow the instructions of his immediate chief—the editor or the chief reporter—or it may be left, as it is in many cases, largely to his own discretion. A meeting may turn out to be more or less important than was originally anticipated, and unless some discretionary power is placed in the reporter's hands the space occupied may be very disproportionate to the actual requirements.

If a meeting has to be condensed to one-half or two-thirds of the length of a verbatim report, a judicious reporter should be able to give his readers all the facts and arguments adduced very much in the words of the speakers themselves, omitting only the repetitions and the unnecessary verbiage which characterize the great majority of spoken addresses. A public speaker is naturally more diffuse than he would be if communicating his thoughts in writing. A reader can look back at a paragraph the sense of which he has missed, but a listener has no such resource, and he therefore expects that the speaker addressing him should be full and explicit in his declarations. The reporter, in his work of condensation, may often be helped, both in matter and style, by thinking what the speaker would have written had he been using his pen instead of his tongue. In regard to length, it may be safely asserted that, as a general rule, a speech may be condensed to three-fourths or two-thirds of its entire length without missing a single idea contained in it. Some speeches, it is true, are so terse and pointed in style as to be incapable of this kind of treatment, but these are very exceptional.

Where the condensation is of a severer kind, involving the rejection, not simply of superfluous verbiage, but of the less material parts of a speech, and the retention of its salient features, a still greater demand is made upon the judgment and discretion of the reporter. Some excellent Shorthand writers, no doubt from the want of experience in this particular branch of reporting work, find it difficult and perplexing. Accustomed to transcribe punctiliously every syllable they have taken down, they cannot endure the thought of extensive omissions such as are often needed in newspaper reporting. There is a time-honored story, *ben trovato* if not *vero*, of a *Times* reporter, on being desired by the editor to cut down a speech to one-half its length, innocently inquired which half he should write. I have hardly ever met with so perfect a specimen of the stenographer pure and simple; but I have known many a young reporter who, in trying to condense a long speech, has laboriously begun at the beginning, dropping a few words here and there, afraid to skip entire sentences, and retaining a large portion of what, after all, has been mere introductory matter leading up to the substantial part of the address; so that when this has been reached he has discovered, to his dismay, that he has used up all the space allotted to him, and, unless he begins *de novo*, he has to dismiss the really important part of the speech in a few lines. The substance of a speech is often summed up at the end in a few words by the speaker himself; and if the reporter has been wise enough to take them down he cannot, as a rule, do better than adopt them for his own abridgment.

This opens up an important and interesting question, viz., how much a reporter should take down of a speech of which he knows that only a condensed report will be required. For a perfect and ideal condensation a reporter should perhaps have before him a verbatim report of the speaker's words. But this involves a great deal of labor alike in the original note-taking and in going through a mass of almost useless material to pick out the parts that alone are needed for the condensed report. The reporter is often able, in listening to a speech, to jot down its chief characteristics and all its telling points, without the necessity of taking a full note. In this case, when he comes to transcribe, the greater part of the mental work of selection has been already accomplished, and all that remains to be done is to give it verbal shape. The labor of wading through a dozen or twenty pages of notes in search of "points" is thus saved. But that is not the only view of the question. It is not *always* possible to decide during the delivery of a speech what the really important points may prove to be. A seemingly insignificant remark, which the reporter has not thought it necessary to note, may turn out to have a very important bearing on the general argument or statement; and it is not until the speaker has concluded that the different parts of his address reveal their true relations and proportions. From this point of view a careful reporter will often prefer to take a very full, I do not mean verbatim, report of a speech of which he knows that only a brief summary will be required. This will be especially the case when the speech is one of unusual importance, such as that of a leading statesman dealing with an interesting political question. There is no doubt a great deal of common-place reporting that hardly calls for this extra exertion on the part of the reporter; and, indeed, the pressure under which reporting is commonly done almost forbids the expenditure of time which such a method involves. But in no case should the reporter content himself with taking down just so much of a speech as he expects to require for his condensed report. Without troubling himself to take a verbatim note, he should take enough to preserve the general drift of the speech, if only that he may be able the better to *describe* its purport, though he may not need even to summarize it in the ordinary way. It is much better that he should throw away a certain amount of labor in useless note-taking than run the risk of missing something which, at first appearing immaterial, acquires importance from a later part of the speech, or from some comment of a subsequent speaker. Much, naturally, will depend on the degree of condensation required and the time at the disposal of the reporter.

Condensation is not the only art which the reporter has to cultivate in reporting speeches. Even when taking a full, or so-called verbatim, speech he soon discovers that a slavish adherence to the speaker's words is out of the question. Different views are taken by different reporters as to how far they are justified in departing from the precise phraseology employed by a speaker. There are, unquestionably, some speakers whom no reporter in his senses would dream of reporting literally. The style is so incoherent, the grammar so loose, and the general construction so involved, that nothing less than a verbal transformation is needed before the words are presented to the public in a printed form. Long sentences have to be broken up, and short ones amalgamated, redundancies lopped off, hiatuses supplied, and a confused, jerky, obscure speech made to read smoothly, easily and intelligibly. Nor is this always an easy task, even to the practised hand. If such a speech happens to deal with statistics, or with any subject of a complicated character or requiring great precision of expression, the labor involved in preparing it for the press is very great, and, when the greatest care has been exercised, the result is often unsatisfactory. It is useless to say that such persons should not be allowed to speak in public, or that if they do they should not be reported. It is enough to know that they do speak, and that sometimes they must be reported. These efforts are among the painful duties of the reporter, and must be accepted together with the easier and more agreeable parts of his professional occupation.

Some speakers are so hopelessly involved, rarely completing a single sentence, that the task of the reporter in dealing with their speeches is by no means an easy one, and, as I have said, nothing short of a complete reconstruction will suffice to render them intelligible. A speaker of this class will begin a sentence two or three times before making a start, then suddenly draw up and make a plunge in another direction, then double back for a moment, then dive into the thickets of a never-ending parenthesis, then wander about in a maze, and finally land in a region of impenetrable obscurity. Half an hour's "turn" at oratory of this description in its most aggravated form is simply maddening. I have sometimes heard a speaker begin after this fashion :—

"This resolution which has been moved by my friend on my right—I wish he was always on my right, for he is a kind of man—you know what I mean —I am always glad, and so is everybody that knows him as well as I do— we went to school together I don't know how many years ago, and I don't want to remember—I was about to say that the principles which we are met this evening are principles that no one, not even the lady who has just spoken—and we are delighted to see ladies on the platform; how we should get on without them I am sure—well, I suppose they could not get on without us either, for you know Milton says, or if it is not Milton, I am not quite sure, but as we advance in life our memory doesn't improve; at least that is my experience—"

and so on. Fortunately such meaningless talk can generally be omitted; but when a reporter has to supply, perhaps for official purposes, a verbatim report, or what is understood to be such, and has to deal with material of this description, he is tempted to bewail his fate. There are no consecutive ideas; there is nothing that is capable of condensation; and if he gives any report at all—a verbatim one is out of the question—he must draw upon his own resources, and make the best guess he can as to what the speaker might, could, would, or should have said.

Other speakers, however, speak with so much precision and deliberation that the reporter has nothing to do but faithfully to record and literally transcribe the words, as an amanuensis would do in the case of ordinary dictation. But this is a rare experience. If it were a common one, the reporter's occupation would be one of the easiest, requiring little more than mechanical skill. Perhaps it is fortunate that it is not so. Difficult speeches, whether in point of speed or of verbal construction, demand the services of highly skilled reporters, and this naturally affects the important question of remuneration. Between the two extremes that I have mentioned there are many gradations to be dealt with according to the necessities of the case, or according to the discretion of the reporter. I have said that a reporter may sometimes be guided in his transcript by his view of what a speaker would have written instead of spoken. This is especially the case when he is summarising or considerably abbreviating. If he is presenting a full report, I do not think that he should always or often adopt this standard. If the speech reads fairly well as delivered, there is no necessity to embellish or reconstruct it—a process which might destroy its character as a *speech*. The reporter is not called upon to convert a speech into an essay. He should, of course, correct any obvious slip or grammatical blunder, and make the words read with reasonable smoothness and accuracy, not omitting to preserve any individual characteristics of the speaker which they may exhibit.

It is the custom of most newspapers to turn the reports of speeches that are not given verbatim, or nearly so, into the third person, at the same time changing the present tense into the past. It is generally assumed that where the first person is used in the report the speech is fully rendered, and the use of the third person is an indication that the address is more or less summarised. But I see no objection to the use of the first person in connection with a moderate degree of condensation. It is more satisfactory to be able to use the speaker's own words than to be changing the person and the tense with every sentence. The change indeed may at times involve some ambiguity, which can only be avoided by the addition of words never used, or the complete reconstruction of the sentence. It also necessitates the frequent insertion of the speaker's name in a parenthesis—as "he (Mr. Briggs) was of opinion"—in order to identify the "he" with the speaker instead of with some other person just mentioned. And where two or three persons are concerned in a narrative, including the speaker himself, this method of discrimination, though absolutely necessary, is apt by its frequent repetition to become extremely awkward and unpleasant. In France it is the custom in changing from the first person to the third to preserve the present tense instead of changing it to the imperfect. Thus, the words, "I am glad to be present at this discussion, and will do my best to make myself heard," instead of being reported as in England, "He was glad to be present at that discussion, and would do his best to make himself heard," would be rendered, "He is glad to present at this discussion, and will do his best to make himself heard." The same method is adopted in the minutes that are made of proceedings before committees of the House of Lords, when the *ipsissima verba* of the speakers are not given. Everything is in the present tense. Thus, "the chairman *states*," "the room *is* cleared," "the parties *are* informed," etc. It was no doubt this peculiarity that once led a member of the House of Lords to declare that if reporters were chronicling the Deluge they would change the past tense into the present. In the House of Commons the corresponding minutes are given in the past tense, as in ordinary English newspaper reporting. The reason for the difference I leave to others to explain. The use of the "historic present" is common enough in ordinary composition; and a good deal may be said for its use in reporting. It involves fewer changes in the speaker's words, and prevents the ambiguity sometimes arising from the changes of present to imperfect, imperfect to perfect, "this" to "that," "now" to "then," and the like, which the most experienced reporters occasionally find embarrassing.

The extent to which the present tense is changed in third person reports depends upon the discretion of the reporter or upon the custom of his paper. The practice is not uniform. The words, "Every one knows that the sun always shines," might be rendered, "Every one knew that the sun always shone," or "Every one knew that the sun always shines." There is no absolute rule on the subject. The great object should be to render the report intelligible to the reader. Some reporters prefer to change the tenses throughout the entire sentence. Others retain the present tense as far as possible. With the latter the words, "The *Times* states that Mr. Jones is of opinion that the country will be flooded," would be rendered, "The *Times stated,*" etc., no further change being made. With the former the sentence would be transcribed, "The *Times* stated that Mr. Jones *was* of opinion that the country *would be* flooded."

The change of "we" into "they" in this style of reporting is often objectionable, especially at the beginning of a speech or a sentence. A speaker says, "We have been delighted to listen to the hon. member for Bristol." Some reporters would transcribe, "*They* had been delighted," etc. I should prefer, "*The meeting* had been delighted," etc. There is no antecedent to "they," and if some other word can be employed in such a case, it is certainly preferable. In such a sentence as, "We are all mortal," there need be no change of tense in a third person report. The words may stand as they are, or be rendered, "We were all mortal," which, I think, is a better rendering than "They were all mortal." It has been said, and I think with reason, that a statement which is "true for all time" need not have a change of tense in a third person report.

A ludicrous effect is sometimes produced by a change of

tense in familiar sayings and quotations. It is said that a reporter once took notes of a speech in which occurred Tennyson's familiar lines,

> "Kind hearts are more than coronets,
> And simple faith than Norman blood,"

which he prosaically rendered, "Kind hearts were more than coronets, and simple faith was superior to Norman blood." The fact that it was an after-dinner performance may perhaps be pleaded as an "extenuating circumstance."

Some writers have taken a very wide view of a reporter's functions in connection with the alterations which he is not only entitled but called upon to make in the speeches which he reports. It has been suggested that a reporter should present to the reader not what the speaker has said, but what he ought to have said, even to the extent of correcting inaccuracies of statement, statistical, historical, scientific, and the like. This would make the reporter responsible for the accuracy of all that he writes, and would involve an amount of general knowledge that is fearful to contemplate. Happily, no such superhuman duty attaches to the reporter's calling. I do not say that he should never correct what he knows to be an error, say in a date, a quotation, an historical reference, or any casual inaccurate statement on which no argument is founded. But he is not bound to do so unless the error be an obvious slip of the tongue. He may do it out of good nature or out of consideration for the speaker; but even then he must be cautious how far he allows his friendly office to extend. The error may have been noticed by others; subsequent speakers may refer to it; or some listener may send a correction to the paper, which, if inserted, will appear meaningless beside the report. Discretion, therefore, must be exercised in the correction of inaccuracies. As a rule speakers themselves should take the responsibility of them, and the reporter should be free to note down and transcribe what he hears, subject to the modifications as to style, etc., which I have already indicated. As to making any addition to a speaker's remarks with a view of completing an argument, or illustrating a point, that I take to be wholly out of the question. A story is told of a Parliamentary reporter once interpolating in a speech a long classical quotation which he thought appropriate. But although, in this particular instance the speaker in republishing the speech, adopted the quotation as his own, and was perhaps grateful for the illustration which it afforded, the practice is not to be commended. It might be resented as an officious intrusion, and lead to unpleasant consequences. It is probably needless to insist on this, since, as a rule, reporters find quite enough to do in recording and transcribing what has actually been said without making gratuitous additions. Indeed, I should hardly have referred to it, had I not known instances in which reporters have been fond of introducing ornamental flourishes into very prosaic utterances, which I am sure must have surprised the speakers themselves, not less than the readers who happened to be familiar with their style.

CHAPTER IX.

Public Meetings.

ONE of the most frequent duties that fall to the lot of the reporter is that of attending and reporting public meetings. Some are almost exclusively so engaged; but as I have already remarked, it forms, in the majority of cases, only a part, of course an important part, of their ordinary engagements. Public meetings are as widely varied as the classes of whom they are composed. One day the reporter may find himself at a Convocation of Bishops, and the next at an indignation meeting of costermongers. A Lord Mayor's feast may alternate (happily for his digestion) with a tea-meeting in Zion Chapel, "tickets, sixpence each." There is absolutely no kind of public gathering to which he is a stranger. Sometimes he is present on sufferance; but generally he is a recognised functionary, and is accommodated accordingly. At an ordinary meeting for the delivery of speeches, a table is usually provided in front of the platform, between the speakers and the audience, sometimes on the platform itself, and to this all duly authorised reporters are admitted. If the occasion is an important one there will be a run upon the seats, and the prudent reporter will take care to be early at his post so as to secure a good position, facing the speakers, not sitting with his back to them. This is especially desirable when several reporters are working together. The members of a small corps should occupy contiguous seats, which should, if possible, be secured sometime beforehand. It may happen that the number of seats provided is insufficient. The first comers naturally possess themselves of them, while their less prudent brethren have to shift for themselves as best they may. Every disposition is generally shown by the managers to accommodate them; but chairs and tables cannot always be extemporised, and a reporter sitting on the corner of a stool, or on a step, with his note-book on his knee, or even standing in a surging crowd and taking notes under trying circumstances, is not by any means an unfamiliar spectacle. The best seat is generally in the middle of the table facing the chairman. In some cases the reporters' tables are placed at the sides instead of in front of the platform. This is a very inconvenient arrangement, especially if any of the seats are behind the speakers—a position which every reporter should always do his best to avoid, involving as it does, considerable difficulty in hearing. Better a dozen yards in front than two yards behind.

It will be impossible to refer in these pages to every kind of meeting requiring the services of a reporter; but a few of the most frequent and most important may be mentioned.

First there is the political meeting. The borough or county member comes to address his constituency and give an account of his stewardship. Or a cabinet minister has promised to address a public meeting on some burning question of the day. Or a big gathering is held to promote some popular political movement, and a batch of celebrities is expected. On all such occasions newspaper men are considerably in evidence. All the papers in the district, and many from a distance, as well as the principal press agencies, are represented, and scores of busy pens are at work chronicling the speeches as they are delivered. In regard to political speeches generally, if the speaker occupies a front rank, to whatever party he may belong, it is customary to report him fully, if not verbatim. Minor speakers are dealt with according to circumstances; party papers giving prominence to men of their own side, and dismissing the others with a few lines. The reporter, in exercising whatever discretion may be entrusted to him, will look to the general interests and views of his paper, and not be guided by any political predilection of his own. If he is a strong politician, he may wince under the necessity of giving prominence to one of the enemy's camp, and keeping his own favorites in the background. But the born reporter is not a party politician; and it is to him a matter of supreme indifference (unless he is paid by quantity) whether he expands a speech to three or four columns or condenses it into as many lines. Conservative and Liberal, Gladstonian and Unionist, are but verbal expressions; apart from his "copy" they are meaningless. As he writes, he is each and all in turns. He abandons his own identity, and merges it into that of the speaker. He is for the time possessed, if not "obsessed," and gives forth as he receives. Nor does he at all suffer from these rapid transitions; they become natural to him. When he is at work it is as much his duty to sink his own individuality as it is in the case of the barrister when he is representing his clients. I know that this doctrine is sometimes pushed to an unwarrantable extreme, and made to justify a political writer in writing in direct violation of his own convictions. The cases are not parallel. The reporter does not make himself responsible for what he writes; he is professedly but a mouth-piece, a narrator. The other assumes the function of a teacher and a guide.

There is no special difficulty in the reporting of political speeches as far as their general matter is concerned. They deal with the current and well known topics of the day, involving no technicalities of a difficult nature. For this reason they are more easily reported than most other forms of public address. No doubt they require great care, especially in the case of official declarations by persons in responsible positions. Such persons generally weigh their words carefully, and as they are sure to be eagerly scrutinized, the reporter cannot be too careful in reproducing them. It is mainly in the matter of finance and statistics that some difficulty now and then arises. Few speakers acquire the art of making figures intelligible; and when a slip is made and is sought to be corrected, the probability is that the confusion is intensified. The reporter should do his best in such cases to obtain a copy of the figures to guide him in his transcript.

Should it be necessary to divide the work of reporting into "turns," the leader of the corps will arrange a time table, which all the members should strictly keep. As I have before explained, the object should be to get all hands to work as quickly as possible, and with this view a few very short turns should be arranged at the beginning, lengthening them, if necessary, later on, but shortening them again towards the end, if it is essential that the copy should be very promptly supplied. These arrangements must largely depend upon the number of hands available.

The religious or philanthropic meeting affords frequent occasion for the exercise of the reporter's craft. The secular press does not ordinarily devote much space to these gatherings; but they fill many pages of newspapers devoted to such movements. After the chairman's speech there is commonly a "report" read by the secretary, giving an account of the labors of the particular society during the year; and of this the reporter should give his readers a good summary. It is often printed beforehand, and copies are distributed among the reporters; or, better still, a convenient abstract is prepared for their use, in which all the salient points are brought out. One of the first features to be noted is, the income and expenditure of the society, showing whether there has been an increase or a decrease in comparison with the previous year. If it be a missionary society, the number of workers, European and native, should be chronicled, the principal scenes of their labors indicated, and any striking fact connected with them recorded. Of late years there has been a marked tendency towards a considerable abbreviation of the long and sometimes prosy narratives which formerly ushered in an annual missionary meeting, their place being now taken by a short summary *spoken*, not read, by the secretary, thus leaving more time for succeeding speeches. There are few things more systematically "scamped" by reporters, especially in London, than meetings of this character. A few lines of the chairman's speech are followed by a hastily written summary of the annual report, and then a line or two stating that the meeting was then addressed by so-and-so, the names being copied from a printed list of expected speakers. This is all that the reader is permitted to know about the meeting. Those who are in the secret understand it well enough. The reporter wants to get away as quickly as possible. If it is a day meeting he probably wants a short report for an evening paper, and every minute is of importance. If it is an evening meeting, the sooner his copy is in the printers' hands the better. The result is that many a speaker, not previously announced, is not even mentioned in the report, while others who have failed to attend find their names recorded in the list of actual speakers. It is assumed that the printed program will be adhered to, and the newspaper paragraph is drafted accordingly. Whatever excuse there may be for the metropolitan reporter, who may be paid by "linage" (of which more anon) and who may be anxious to secure the insertion of his paragraph by prompt delivery, there is not the same extenuation to be offered for the country reporter who slips away from a meeting at an early period and runs the risk of making an awkward blunder as to the subsequent proceedings.

The mistake may not be so serious in its consequences as that of the dramatic critic who, after severely criticising an actor's performance, discovered to his cost that the subject of his criticism had been taken ill and had not performed at all. But even slight errors should be avoided, and nothing should be assumed as having happened, simply because it is part of a printed programme.

Companies' meetings, especially in London and the larger cities of the Empire, are of frequent occurrence, and are usually reported in the papers. A few only are held in private, reporters who do not happen to be shareholders not being admitted. Unless there is some special reason for giving a full report of a Company's meeting throughout—as when any serious defalcations have to be announced—the method usually adopted is to report the chairman's speech in full (not necessarily verbatim) and the other speeches very briefly. The yearly; or half-yearly report on these occasions is of course a very important document, but it is generally printed and distributed a week or two beforehand, and, in the case of railway and other large companies, is published in the papers in anticipation of the meeting, so that it is unnecessary to repeat it with the report of the speeches. But where this has not been done it is essential to give its main features, showing the annual income and expenditure, the nature and amount of the traffic or other business, the amount of the proposed dividend, and other matters of general interest. The young reporter may find some difficulty at first in dealing with these financial and business matters; and he will be wise to note how they are treated by other and more experienced hands. In London there are class papers specially devoted to reporting meetings of this description, which occur every week, if not every day, in the year, and afford a wide field for the reporter's labors. In other places they are of less frequent occurrence, but they are rarely altogether absent from the reporter's diary. In attending one of these periodical gatherings, the reporter should make a point at once of securing a copy of the annual report and of any other documents that are being distributed, and he cannot better utilise the few minutes that he has to spare before the proceedings begin, than by glancing through their pages and making himself generally acquainted with their contents. This will probably assist him in his work, familiarising him with the names of persons and places mentioned, and enabling him to understand allusions in the speeches which, but for such aid, might be almost unintelligible. This is the more desirable since it is not now the custom to read annual reports of business meetings, which, as their contents are well-known to the shareholders, are commonly "taken as read." Under any circumstances, the reporter should have the document by his side for reference while he is writing out his report.

There is a feature in connection with shareholders' meetings which sometimes presents a little difficulty to the reporter. I refer to the circumstance that the speeches are not made from a platform, but from different parts of the room, the speakers rising from their places, and no announcement being made of their name. Sometimes, indeed, a lively discussion is carried on between a shareholder and the chairman, or between two or more shareholders, whose names may be unknown to the reporter, who is in a state of considerable perplexity as to how to distinguish them. If he leaves off writing to inquire the names he may miss something material. An unknown speaker is sometimes described as "a shareholder," and if a second and third follow, the reporter can only write them "another shareholder." But when they begin talking to one another, this method of designation becomes extremely awkward, and the young reporter is thrown on his beam ends. The reporters at these meetings usually sit at the directors' table, and it often happens that the chairman or the secretary or one of the directors will be able to give the required information. The chairman will sometimes, if requested, make a point of announcing the name of each speaker as he rises, and if he is not known, will ask him to state it; but when the discussion becomes exciting or conversational this is altogether forgotten, and the reporter is left to his own devices. He should never forget in these cases to write at least some distinguishing mark to show that a new speaker has risen. He cannot do better than draw a circle at the left side of the page within which he can write the name as soon as he knows it, which may be within a few seconds. It is also a good plan in such cases to write some simple word which will serve to recall the speaker later on when making inquiries, say after the meeting is at an end. An extemporised appellation, as "white tie," "green spectacles," "bald," "stout," "long-beard," may prove a convenient means of identification, and save the reporter a good deal of embarrassment. Where several reporters are engaged, a speaker may be known to one of them, and not to the others, and no one but a churl will refuse to give the required information, if he possesses it, to his brethren.

Meetings of Town Councils, Boards of Guardians, and statutory meetings of various kinds come frequently under the cognizance of the reporter. In such assemblies an "agenda paper" is often printed before-hand, and with this before him the reporter is placed *au courant* with the different items of business to be dealt with. Some experience is needed as to their method of treatment, distinguishing the substantial from the merely formal, and apportioning the space at command to the various subjects discussed according to their relative importance. The young hand will probably find himself taking elaborate notes while his colleagues are sharpening their pencils or quietly studying the agenda paper, and will afterwards discover that he has been giving himself needless labor. But that is not a serious matter. It is better to do too much note-taking than too little. Experience will soon teach the reporter how, in this as in other respects, to economise his strength; and he will learn to smile, in his turn, at the superfluous energy displayed by his younger brothers. The speakers at the meetings to which I am referring being, to a certain extent, permanent or regular members of the body, soon become known to the reporter who is in the habit of attending, and there is therefore little or no difficulty with regard to names.

Festivals of every description naturally come within the scope of the reporter's avocations. No public dinner is complete without the presence of "the Press." Tickets are usually sent to the newspapers in the district, but where these are very numerous a selection is made, and only one or two of the principal journals are invited to send representatives. Some friction has occasionally arisen in consequence of invitations being sent to the reporters to attend *after dinner* and report the speeches. This is almost always, and very properly resented; and many speeches have suffered the fate of the "unreported Parliament" owing to the scant courtesy shown to the reporters. In the majority of cases a dinner, like a conversazione, means evening dress, and a reporter should not cast discredit upon his calling by appearing in any other attire, unless he knows that the *grande tenue* is optional or not expected, as in the case of small and unimportant gatherings. Attention to these details should never be neglected if the reporter would maintain the social position to which his profession should entitle him. The reporters' seats are usually grouped at one of the tables at no great distance from the chairman's; but occasionally they are relegated to a very inconvenient corner where hearing is a matter of difficulty. If the arrangement cannot be altered, the reporter who has to take a full note of the speeches will do well, after dinner, to shift his quarters, and find a convenient corner at another table where he can hear and write at ease. With a little address this can generally be managed, and it will greatly facilitate his labors. If, however, he has only a brief report to supply, he may content himself with the place assigned to him.

It is usual to give a list of the principal persons attending a public festival. This can be obtained from the secretary or other officials, or from the cards which will be found on the plates at the principal tables, containing the names of the visitors. In the case of large and important gatherings a plan of the dinner table is printed and distributed, showing the position of every guest; and this is a convenience which every reporter will appreciate. It is sometimes accompanied by an alphabetical list of names, showing the number of the table and the seat assigned to each visitor, who thus knows, on entering, where to betake himself.

It is not customary to report at length the "loyal toasts" at a public dinner. These are yearly becoming shorter and shorter, and are sometimes consolidated into a single comprehensive toast proposed from the chair. The "Church" is occasionally omitted altogether, and the "Army and Navy" now and then meets with no better fate. The chief reason for their retention in the toast-list is that it affords the opportunity of a speech or two from some of the guests in attendance, to whom it is desired to pay a compliment.

The speech to which special attention should be given by the reporter is that which proposes what is known as "the toast of the evening." This is always proposed from the chair, and it contains a statement of the object or objects sought to be promoted by the entertainment. If it is a hospital, or other charity, the statistics connected with it—its income and expenditure, the character and number of its beneficiaries, and the like,—are presented, and a general appeal is made for the promotion of the enterprise. If it is a complimentary dinner, the chief toast is, of course, devoted to the guest of the evening, whose reply, as well as the speech of the proposer, usually receives special prominence in the report.

May I give a word of counsel to the young reporter to whom the attractions of a public festival are likely to prove a temptation? I do not say that in the majority of cases a glass or two of wine will interfere with the work of the evening, but the quantity should be *strictly limited*, and if there is any felt tendency to undue indulgence, entire abstinence should be followed. An abstaining reporter was, within my own recollection, a *rara avis*, but the genus is now common enough, and no dread of singularity need deter the débutant from passing on the wine-bottle and contenting himself with seltzer or apollinaris. I have known many a report spoiled by a yielding to the terrible fascinations of the champagne bottle, and many a promising career in connection with journalism hopelessly destroyed from the same cause. The opportunities of indulgence are so frequent that the utmost caution should, be exercised, and, when found to be needful, absolute abstention practised. I should not feel that I had discharged my duty to my younger brethren if I had not brought this matter strongly before them.

At the annual summer meetings of scientific, religious, and other associations that manage to mingle business and pleasure in their peripatetic assemblies, abundant occupation is afforded to the reporting fraternity. A meeting like that, for example, of the British Association at some county town where reporters are not numerous, often puts a heavy strain upon newspaper resources, and necessitates the calling in of extraneous help from other quarters. The reason is, that not only are the meetings held continuously, extending over several days, but they are divided into numerous sections which sit concurrently, and each section requires the services of at least one reporter. Occasionally several papers in a district unite their forces under these circumstances, exchanging "proofs" of the different sections; but where a paper has a large staff at its disposal, it often prefers a perfectly independent report. The difficulty of reporting the proceedings of these bodies varies greatly. Some of the sections may deal with subjects of so highly abstruse or technical a character that only an expert can satisfactorily report them. Nor would a report, however accurate, be of much interest to the general public. Newspaper readers do not largely concern themselves about "the kinetic stability of equilibrium with electro-magnetic forces," or "the history of Plaff's Problem." The result is that topics of this character rarely find their way into newspaper columns, and the reporters simply chronicle the fact that such and such papers were read and discussed. Other sections, however, devoted to subjects of more popular interest, are reported at more or less length. They are commonly introduced by a paper, of which an abstract, sometimes prepared by the author himself, is available for the use of the reporters, but this cannot always be relied upon, and it may therefore be necessary to take a note of the paper as it is being read. Not unfrequently the paper is printed in full, and copies are usually distributed to the press. The reporter can then insert it bodily in his report if it is sufficiently important and is not too long, or can condense it into suitable proportions. Where such reports can be obtained a day or two beforehand, a good deal of the work can be prepared in anticipation, and I need not say that in cases of heavy pressure this should always be done wherever it is practicable. With regard to the opening address of the President, it is almost invariably in type some time in advance, and copies are supplied to the newspapers before it is delivered; it is therefore needless to report it in shorthand. But reporters should never rely upon aid of this kind being forthcoming unless it is a matter of absolute certainty. I have often known an expectation of this character disappointed, and the reporter having taken no note as a matter of precaution, he has had no materials whatever for a report unless he has been able to obtain them from others who have acted with greater prudence.

Religious gatherings, like the Church Congress and the Congregational Union, also meet at times in sections, and the principal papers read and discussed at them are printed beforehand and copies distributed. Or it may happen that a particular newspaper has obtained certain of the manuscripts for its own use, and if the editor or reporter is reasonable and good-natured, the reporters for other papers may secure "slips" or "proofs" of such as they may need for their own reports. The interchange of courtesies of this kind is happily very common among newspapers, and it should always be practised and encouraged whenever it is possible. It minimizes labor and promotes harmony and general convenience.

The legislation of the last ten or fifteen years has added greatly to the reporting work throughout the country, and this has naturally led to a considerable increase in the staffs of most of the provincial papers. A number of public bodies have been called into existence by statutory enactment, and their proceedings are of a nature calling for a more or less detailed report. The County Councils are perhaps among the most important of these newly constituted authorities. Like Town Councils, they meet quarterly and sometimes oftener. In many counties the Joint Committees (of County Councillors and Justices), which deal with police administration, are open to the press. The old Courts of Quarter Sessions for County business are deprived of most of their functions; but they still hold meetings for certain purposes, and, of course, sit in a judicial capacity. District or Parish Councils have not yet been created by Parliament; but they are probably in the near future, and, when established, they will greatly extend the field of the reporter's labors. Even the more important Committees of some of these local bodies, municipal or otherwise, are occasionally open to the press. This is especially the case with the big spending Committees of Town Councils, in which the public as rate-payers have a special interest; and the practice seems to be growing.

On many of the smaller provincial papers, reporters are expected to assist in sub-editing. Indeed, the two functions of reporter and sub-editor are sometimes combined in one individual; and cases are not unknown—happily, they are rare—in which the editorial duties are thrown in. It is generally supposed that the sub-editor's work is limited to the judicious use of "scissors and paste." This is hardly the case. Where there is a large staff of local correspondents, their copy will entail a great amount of labor in condensation and emendation, often to the extent of entire reconstruction. Daily papers and the larger weekly journals usually have an independent sub-editorial staff; but, in case of necessity, a reporter is called to assist in this department, with which, therefore, every "all round" journalist should have some familiarity.

CHAPTER X.

Legal Proceedings.

LEGAL proceedings afford ample scope for the reporter's pen. They are rather trying to the beginner, and need a good deal of care and some special experience if satisfactory reports are to be produced. Mistakes in this class of reporting are easily made, and are more likely to be serious in their character and consequences than in any other kind of journalistic work. An action for libel may be readily fastened on an apparently simple and innocent error, and too much caution cannot be exercised to prevent any such contingency, which may cost the reporter his situation and inflict serious pecuniary loss on his employers.

The Police Court is often the scene of the junior reporter's labors. A good deal of the business brought before it is commonly of a very simple character, requiring no great skill on the part of the reporter. But, especially in large cities, very important cases are sometimes heard before these tribunals, involving nice points of law, and needing the utmost care in presenting the details to the public. The ordinary cases are, as a rule, easily dealt with. A full report is rarely given. The facts of the case are briefly stated in a paragraph form, no attempt being made to give the evidence of the witnesses in detail. Some skill and practice are needed even in this subordinate class of work. The material facts should be clearly grasped and expressed in appropriate language, without needless verbiage, but with clearness and precision. Some reporters exhibit a great facility in these little compositions, and acquire the knack of summing up in a dozen or twenty lines the points of a long case which a less experienced hand would require at least a column to develop to his satisfaction. These brief reports rarely call for the use of Shorthand except for the purpose of jotting down a few notes of the salient points; and the MS. for the printers can generally be prepared as the case proceeds, or in the intervals between the cases, or during the hearing of cases that need no report. In this way, all the copy is ready to be handed in at the rising of the Court, unless anything of unusual importance has arisen calling for a more detailed account. The beginner may find some difficulty in this rapid and concurrent preparation of copy, and he need not be in too great a hurry to acquire it. It will come in due time. Meanwhile, it will be better that he should take needlessly voluminous notes, to be afterwards "boiled down," than run the risk of missing what may turn out to be material and important.

Another tribunal whose proceedings the reporter has from time to time to record is the County Court, whose jurisdiction has been of late years so widely extended as to embrace a large number of cases formerly dealt with only in the superior Courts in the Metropolis and at the periodical Assizes. Many are of a very simple character, relating to some insignificant debt, and involving no detail of the slightest public interest. These are reported with great brevity or wholly ignored. Others, of more importance, are tried with the aid of a jury, and sometimes legal points arise of great nicety and requiring some skill and experience to state them with precision. To familiarize himself with this kind of work, the reporter should accustom himself to read and study legal reports like those given daily in the *Times* or in the authorized "Reports," and the occasional perusal of a legal text-book will assist him greatly in his labors. I have always recommended the young reporter to read Blackstone's Commentaries early in life. The perusal will not only enlarge his knowledge and give him at least a smattering of the general principles of English law, but will enable him the better to deal with whatever legal reporting may fall to his lot. Frequent attendance at Court may answer the same purpose; but this does not fall to the lot of every reporter, and in his early days the opportunities of acquiring practical experience of this kind may be few and far between.

The most important legal tribunals, and those of which the proceedings are most fully reported, are the Supreme Court of Judicature (as the Appellate Courts in London are called) and the High Court of Justice, including the Queen's Bench and Chancery Divisions. The London reporters are the chief practitioners in these; but country reporters are often sent to the Metropolis to report some case of special interest and importance in their own district, and occasionally find themselves ill at ease in the unfamiliar precincts of Carey Street and Chancery Lane. An ordinary civil trial before a Judge and Jury may present no great difficulty even to a comparatively inexperienced hand. But with a case in the Divisional Court or the Court of Appeal, where (as in the old sittings *In Banco* at Westminster or in the Court of Chancery at Lincoln's Inn) the speeches are mainly devoted to the discussion of legal technicalities, a young and unpractised hand, whatever his stenographic acquirements, may, and that without any imputation on his abilities, find himself in a position of utter bewilderment. The novelty of the experience, the rapidity with which the proceedings are conducted, the apparent mutual understandings between judge and counsel, by which half a sentence is made to convey a world of meaning, all obscure, however, to the puzzled novice—these and other difficulties incident to a first visit to the Law Courts have sometimes driven the "young man from the country" wild with distraction, and made him forswear an occupation for which he feels himself hopelessly disqualified. But there is really no solid ground for discouragement. A little experience will familiarize the practitioner with modes of procedure at first so foreign to him, and enable him to seize the points which seem to be flying about in all directions and to elude his grasp. He will soon discover the means of obtaining from the solicitors engaged in his case a few printed or written papers in which the main features are set out and ready to his hand. These, carefully read if possible beforehand and, as far as necessary, noted in his book, will tend to restore his lost equanimity, and enable him to follow the discussions with greater ease. In an ordinary case, the "statement of claim" and the "statement of defence" will give him all the information he needs. If it be the hearing of a petition, a copy of that document is usually available for his inspection, and will save him a world of trouble and anxiety as to names and figures, which are not always brought out clearly by counsel, knowing as he does that the judge has all the details before him. Even with this aid, however, the reporter will find occasion for the exercise of all his faculties. Where there are several parties to a case, a good deal of complication may arise;

and in administration suits, cases dealing with the law of real estate, and the like, technicalities spring up which are a complete mystery to the uninitiated. While in patent cases and others of a similar character the scientific terminology often adds another terror to the "'prentice han'" who has never heard of "pyrogallol," and would tremble in his shoes at hearing a witness discourse of "trioxybenzophenone" or "phenylhydrazine monosulphonic acid."

Many of the cases heard at the Assizes in the country are much of the same character as those tried in the Law Courts in London. Most of them are heard before a judge and jury; but of late years it has become a frequent practice to hear cases involving only questions of law, and not of fact, before the judge alone. Criminal cases are also heard at the Assizes, and these give the reporter much less trouble than cases tried on the "civil side," not often involving the legal subtleties which commonly surround purely legal discussions. The length at which the cases are reported will naturally depend on the public interest likely to attach to them. Unless they are reported very fully, they can generally be "written up" as they proceed. It may be necessary to take a shorthand note of the opening speech of counsel containing an outline of the case; but the evidence can easily be written in longhand, unless, as in very important trials, it is thought desirable to give it in the form of question and answer. The judge usually takes a note of the evidence in narrative form for his own use; this necessitates frequent pauses, and enables the reporter to keep up easily with the evidence. Indeed, as he is probably a more skilful penman than the judge, and moreover avails himself of a large number of press contractions (see page 109), he should be able to write much more rapidly than the judge himself, who confines his attention to the facts that are absolutely material to the issue, and takes no heed of the "public" whose interest the reporter seeks to serve.

In regard to the criminal trials, it may be mentioned that a list of the prisoners is always printed, and copies can be obtained by the reporters. From these can be gathered the name, age, etc. of each prisoner, and the nature and the date of the offence with which he is charged. These details, needed for the opening paragraph of the report, can be written during the preliminary formalities attending the swearing of the jury, and the case can then be reported as it proceeds, giving the evidence of each witness separately, or, as described above, summarizing the whole proceedings in a descriptive paragraph, without any attempt to report the evidence in detail. This is not a difficult task in the case of criminal trials; but, as already explained, in civil proceedings some practice is needed before the work can be satisfactorily accomplished. Objections are often made in the progress of a trial, discussions arise, authorities are cited and judicial decisions given, which are apt to embarrass the unskilled reporter; and the character of the report greatly depends upon the accuracy and lucidity with which these points are stated.* The judge's summing up should be carefully watched, and the general effect of his instructions to the jury duly noted; and any discussions between counsel and the bench after the verdict is given, as to its legality or its effect, should have the reporter's best attention, as they often materially concern the ultimate issue of the case. An occasional shorthand note of these discussions will be found very serviceable, the precise words used being sometimes of the greatest importance. When the case is heard by the judge alone, his decision is given in the form of a "judgment," which in important cases should be carefully taken, and its purport at least presented with scrupulous fidelity. To find, after the publication, the plaintiff's or defendant's solicitor writing to correct some inaccuracy or supply some important omission in the report, is always a mortifying experience, and it can only be avoided by close attention to the case in all its stages. Few reporters perhaps wholly escape it. *Nemo mortalium, &c.* The best reporter, like the best general, is not the one who makes no mistakes, but the one who makes the fewest.

Coroners' Inquests form the material for many a newspaper

---

* A high compliment was once paid to a newspaper reporter for a summary which he had given of a legal trial. One of the litigant parties told the reporter that he had never thoroughly understood the points in dispute before reading the summary in question, which threw so much light upon them that he went straightway to the opposite side, agreed with his adversary quickly, and so terminated what otherwise would have been a prolonged litigation.

paragraph, and sometimes of very full reports. Coroners have the privilege of holding their inquiries in private, but very rarely exercise it, and when they do, the reporters find means of ascertaining from the jury or some of the witnesses the purport of the evidence given. In cases of little public interest, if the reporter has not attended the inquest, he is frequently permitted to read the depositions taken by the coroner and compile his report therefrom.

Government Inquiries are often held in public, and therefore reported by the Press. They are of a *quasi* legal character, the witnesses being examined as in a court of law, but not with the same strictness. They are usually presided over by an Inspector or other official connected with some Government Department, who sends in his report to his superiors. There is no great difficulty in reporting the proceedings either fully or in a condensed form.

Parliamentary Committees during the Session of Parliament furnish abundant material to the newspapers. To these tribunals railway and other "private bills," as they are called, are referred by the two Houses, and many a fierce conflict is waged before them. The Committee usually consists of five members of Parliament, who sit at a long horse-shoe table, in the middle of the inner bend of which a small table is placed for the witness and the official Shorthand writer. The counsel for the different parties concerned occupy another table facing the Committee, and a fourth table at the side is provided for the accomodation of the newspaper reporters. These are as a rule the representatives of country newspapers specially interested in the particular Bill under consideration. They may be sent up to London for the purpose of reporting the proceedings, or (as is more frequently the case) they may be acting in behalf of the different Press Associations or firms in London which supply the provincial press with reports and news of local interest. The counsel for the "promoters," the persons promoting the measure in question, is first heard. He opens the case or the "Bill," a copy of which should be obtained by the reporter; and he then calls his witnesses, who are examined on oath, and cross-examined, as in a court of law. The opponents are called "petitioners," of whom there may be a considerable number, some appearing by counsel and others not. Each petition is printed, setting forth the grounds of the opposition; and copies of these documents will always be useful to the reporter. The "parliamentary agent" takes the place of the attorney in court, and is the person to whom application should be made for copies of documents required. If a full report is needed it must be taken in Shorthand and then transcribed. It is impossible to take the evidence fully in longhand as at an ordinary trial, since there are no pauses required to enable the Committee to take notes for themselves. The presence of an official Shorthand writer renders this unnecessary, his duty being (as will appear in another chapter) to take full notes of every question and answer, and transcribe them for the printer, who supplies copies to the members of the Committee at the commencement of each sitting. But if only a column or so daily is required, longhand will generally suffice both for the evidence and the speeches. At the close of the case the Committee Room is cleared, and the Committee deliberate in private. As soon as they have arrived at a decision the public and the reporters are re-admitted, and the result is duly announced by the chairman. It should be very carefully noted. It is usually to the effect that the "preamble" of the Bill has been "proved" or "not proved;" and sometimes certain conditions are imposed upon the promoters, such as bringing up a clause providing for some claim by a petitioner, and these should of course be given with precision. After the decision of the Committee the clauses of the Bill are considered. This is often a mere formal proceeding and requires no report; but there are occasionally severe contests on clauses, witnesses being examined and speeches made on either side, in which case the reporter's services are still further needed. He should never leave the Committee before ascertaining that all contentious business is at an end. Before the proceedings begin, he should ascertain the names of the Committee, and also of the counsel engaged in the case—information which he can usually obtain from one of the agents or from the "Committee clerk." In the case of what is called a "Select Committee" of either House, or a Joint (or "Hybrid") Committee, consisting of members of both Houses, the numbers are generally larger, from fifteen to twenty or more, and there is greater difficulty in ascertaining and remembering their names. To facilitate this a plan of the table may be drawn indicating the names of the Committee and the places they occupy—thus:—

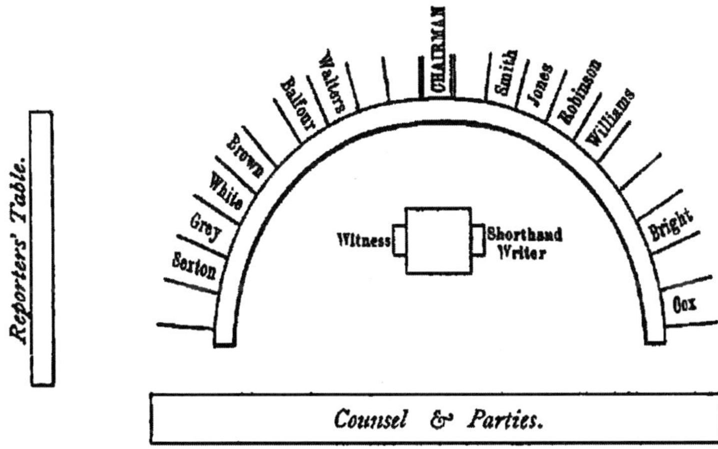

The members generally retain the same seats throughout the inquiry, but this is not always to be relied on, and any changes, temporary or otherwise, should be noted by the reporter, who might otherwise attribute observations to the wrong members. The room is sometimes "cleared" for a short time during the sittings of the committee for the purpose of consultation on some point that has arisen. If it is an important point, there may be a rush of the public or the "parties" when the period of readmission is announced, and the reporter should be in readiness to be among the first admitted, that he may be in his place in time to catch the terms of the decision announced by the chairman.

In enumerating the legal tribunals whose proceedings are reported in the papers, the Bankruptcy Courts must not be forgotten. As in the case of the County Courts (some of which, by the way, have a bankruptcy jurisdiction of their own), the proceedings are, for the most part, of little public interest, and are therefore reported with great brevity. But cases of great importance are sometimes brought before them which call for a more extended report. Their special interest to the reporter himself lies in the circumstance that he is sometimes engaged to take an official Shorthand note of the examinations, for which, of course, he is suitably remunerated. In London, there are permanent official Shorthand writers appointed for this purpose. In provincial towns, the work is usually assigned to the reporters for the Press, who may be the only Shorthand writers available. Their names are on a list kept by the Registrar, and they are called upon in turn to take notes of the evidence and transcribe them for the use of the Court and the parties. Where the sittings are frequent, and the cases are of sufficient importance to justify the employment of a Shorthand writer, the reporters appointed are able in this way to make an acceptable addition to their income. The fees sometimes vary with the amount of the bankrupt's estate, and they are not uniform throughout the country. There is usually an attendance fee of a guinea or half a guinea, or, in very small cases, even less; and a charge of from fourpence to eightpence a folio (90 words, not 72 as in other legal work) is made for the transcript. The smallness of the attendance fees has its compensation in the shortness of the duration of the cases, several being often disposed of in a single day.

CHAPTER XI.

DESCRIPTIVE AND ALL-ROUND WORK.

IN addition to attending and reporting public meetings and the Law Courts, most reporters, at any rate in the provinces, have more or less of descriptive work assigned to them. Some of it comes naturally in connection with the meetings themselves, as when a new building is opened, or when a learned society takes a pleasure trip into the country, and an account has to be written for the papers. At other times the work is purely descriptive, there being no speeches to report, or only a few of the briefest possible character. A review, a ship-launch, an agricultural or horticultural show, a National or International Exhibition, a boat-race, a wedding, a funeral, or even a prize-fight,—anything and everything in which the public, or any considerable section of it, is interested—demands the reporter's services, and needs for the proper fulfilment of his task a certain faculty of observation, a facility of composition, and an amount of general information that are indispensable to the "all-round" press man. The most important work of this class is usually assigned to specially qualified men, and how well the work is generally done in first-class journals every newspaper reader can testify. But even a junior hand may occasionally find himself in a position calculated to call forth whatever descriptive power he may possess.

The first word of advice which I would offer to the reporter who lays himself out for descriptive work, is that he should avoid all attempts at fine writing. I give this a prominent position, because it is a temptation that besets almost every beginner who has, or fancies that he has, any facility of composition. The advice will probably not be followed; but if it only moderates, in a few cases, the early tendency to a display of verbal pyrotechnics, it will serve its purpose. Simplicity and directness of style should be sedulously cultivated, and even the humorous faculty, where it exists, should be kept in check. I do not go so far as some have done, and recommend the young writer, whether as reporter or author, to run his pen through every passage that strikes him as particularly eloquent; but I do, and that very strongly, urge the importance of avoiding the effusive and highly ornate productions which are so often the pride and the delight of the juvenile literary aspirant. A light and graceful style is very suitable for many kinds of newspaper work; but it should be natural and unforced, not affected or strained. In the narration of facts nothing is more appropriate than severe simplicity; and even in such tempting work as descriptions of scenery, and the relation of incidents of a naturally dramatic character, the gush and the glow should be subdued lest, in untrained hands, it should degenerate into bathos. Recognised masters of style like Macaulay, Froude, and Oliver Wendell Holmes, should be read and studied. These, and a few good works on composition, will save the reporter from the perils alike of the slipshod and the grandiose, and enable him to avoid the reproach so often cast on "newspaper English." The reproach is not always deserved. No better English can be desired than that which may be read in the columns of some of our best conducted journals. But in those of an inferior class, examples of composition are too often found which are the terror of cultivated minds. For some further hints on this subject I refer the reader to a subsequent chapter on "Composition."

It is impossible to specify all the classes of public events which it is the reporter's duty to chronicle. Whatever the event be, he should endeavour to obtain his information from the best sources and at the most suitable opportunities. He cannot possibly be an expert in every department of human affairs, and must always depend largely upon the assistance of others. The *ideal* reporter, besides being a skilful stenographer, should perhaps be a politician, a theologian, a scientist, an artist, a poet, a statistician, a sportsman, a philologist, an historian, a political economist, a linguist, in short a walking, breathing encyclopedia. As the *actual* reporter is not likely to reach this standard, he must often, like the barrister with his brief, content himself with being "crammed" for the occasion. It is said that a statesman should be able to adapt himself to any position into which he may be thrust by the exigencies of his party. Thus a man who does not know a studding-sail from a marlin-spike, or the futtocks from the keelson, may find himself the First Lord of the Admiralty and the "the ruler of the Queen's Navee." In like manner, the newspaper reporter who has never been on the grand stand in his life, may have to chronicle a horse race and speak learnedly of fillies and three-year-olds, and the latest scratchings. Or, as innocent as a babe of architecture, he may be under the necessity of describing a new church, and exhibiting the familiarity of an expert with "perpendicular" and "early English," with "gargoyles" and "finials." What he needs for his professional purposes is a general idea of *what questions to ask*, a readiness of apprehension and assimilation, and a reasonable facility of expression. If he knows but little of his subject, he will be careful not to commit himself or his paper to any positive opinions on what appear to be disputed points, and confine himself as far as possible to historical narrative and general description. The "crammer" if a partizan or a "fad," will soon reveal his character, and the prudent reporter, while listening attentively, will decline to be led into his informant's groove, and will learn how to separate matters of fact from matters of mere opinion. Whatever printed or written books or documents are available should be obtained, beforehand if possible, and duly scanned. Secretaries and other officials, if properly approached, are generally ready and willing to assist accredited reporters to the best of their ability; and to place himself on good terms with the constituted authorities, should be the aim of every reporter who desires to be placed *au courant* with the facts and incidents which he has to weave into his narrative. To accomplish this, a good address, a modest gentlemanly demeanor and tact are the main essentials. The pushing, fussy, self-asserting reporter may now and then edge his way where his more retiring brother has remained in the background; but his character will soon be known, and his presence avoided. Extreme bashfulness, is of course, a barrier to successful journalism of any kind. True modesty, however, is quite consistent with energy and determination. It is the happy combination of these qualities that secures the best results in the reporting as, I suppose, in most other professions.

As the reporter acquires experience, he will become less and less dependent upon others for assistance. His daily work will be of itself an education, and if he adds to it as much general reading as his time will permit, he will become every year better qualified for the fulfilment of his numerous and sometimes arduous duties.

In addition to his knowledge of affairs in general, the reporter should make it a point to acquire a perfect familiarity with local geography and history. He should know all about his own district and county, its history, its topography, its antiquities, its geological features, its leading families and the like. His own avocations will constantly give him facilities in this direction; and whatever information he can collect in this way on matters of purely local interest, will assuredly prove serviceable in his professional work. An important event—say a murder, a fire, or a serious accident—occurs somewhere within the area covered by his paper. He has to "write it up," and if, in addition to the general facts that he has ascertained, he is able to give his account a local coloring, and utilize his collected historical or topographical materials, he will greatly add to the interest of his narrative, and distance his competitors who have not made the like provision for the contingency which has arisen. A common-place book, well arranged and indexed, will prove of inestimable value to the newspaper reporter, especially if original and descriptive writing often comes in his way. If it does not give him the information which he seeks it will at least tell him where he can obtain it, and the necessity of long and laborious research will thus be avoided.

In these days of illustrated journalism, a reporter who to his knowledge of shorthand has added some acquaintance with photography, may find ample scope for the practice of the latter art, especially in connection with descriptive work. It may seem too much to expect a reporter to encumber himself in his travels with a photographic camera in addition to his writing materials. And if the only cameras available were those of the ordinary description, the labor involved in their use would be too great for one who had other and more important duties to fulfil. But with the new photographic apparatus, the kodak, the labor is brought down to an almost "irreducible minimum." The instrument is comprised in a small case which can be easily slung over the shoulder, and its mode of working is simplicity itself. It is provided with a number of gelatine films, and the operator has simply to lift a cord, point the camera at the object to be taken, and press a button, and the work is done. The turn of a key removes the film to the back of the kodak and exposes another for the next picture. Then *da capo*. It is needless to dwell upon the advantages of being able to secure an accurate photo of any passing incident of special interest, of a ceremonial, the scene of an accident, a new building, a distinguished person, and the like coming under the reporter's observation in connection with his professional engagements. The principal illustrated journals have, as is well known, special artists of their own who attend on important occasions to sketch their chief incidents. But country papers cannot afford the luxury of special artists. Yet the practice of giving illustrations is increasing. These are of a rough and ready character, and are prepared by "processes" of different kinds, most of them quite inexpensive. When a photograph is taken it only needs to be developed, (which can be done by anyone familiar with the process), and then subjected to one of the many methods of reproduction on a block, which can be inserted among the type and printed with it. I am not suggesting that this double function should be exercised by every reporter, or that the photographic qualification should be considered as in any way essential; but I think there can be no doubt as to the value of this addition to the reporter's accomplishments. Even if he does not need it for his professional purposes, he will find it a source of constant personal interest. I can speak on the subject from some very recent experience. In one of my professional visits to India, I armed myself with a kodak, and though I knew absolutely nothing of its use, and worked with it literally in the dark, I succeeded in taking a considerable number of views of Indian scenery and village life which are of great interest and some value. I believe there are other instantaneous photographic processes; but I can only speak from experience of the kodak, which I have found extremely effective. It is made of various sizes, the smallest (No 1) being that which I took with me to the east.

Many opportunities are presented to the newspaper reporter of adding to his regular income. This is mainly done by contributing items of news to London and other papers, which is usually permitted by newspaper proprietors and editors, so far as it does not interfere with the due fulfilment of the reporter's duties to his own journal. The work is known as "linage," being paid for at so much per line, generally a penny or three half-pence. These contributions are sent direct to the newspapers or to one of the Press Associations, which distributes them to their various clients. Sometimes the reporter is specially instructed to send all items of importance from his locality, but very often, where there is no recognised correspondent, paragraphs are sent on speculation, being paid for only if inserted. It is easy to manifold the "copy" sent, by means of carbonized paper, and the same messages can thus be contributed to various journals. When they are wired the cost of telegraphing is very trifling if spread over a number of copies. The charge for the first message is 1s. for 75 words if sent before six o'clock in the evening, and 1s. per 100 words if forwarded after that hour. But the copies are sent at the reduced rate of 2d. per 100 words. Many private engagements also come in the reporter's way if he is an efficient shorthand writer. Special reports of lectures, meetings, sermons and the like are occasionally needed, especially in large towns, and no one is so likely to receive the commission as a good newspaper reporter if he is available for the purpose. Local arbitrations and inquiries also occasionally fall in his way; and if he is able to undertake them, they are a source of considerable profit. If the work is too heavy for a single hand, the reporter who receives the commission can call in the aid of his colleagues, who are generally ready and willing to assist in work of the kind, if they are reasonably remunerated.

When a reporter in a particular district is the accredited correspondent of certain journals or agencies, it is usual for his confrères to recognize his position, and not seek to supplant him by underbidding or sending news in the way of competition. A good deal of ill-feeling has arisen in consequence of attempts to violate this very wholesome professional usage, and the Institute of Journalists has been appealed to on the subject, with the result that the following code has been drawn up by the Council for the guidance of its members:—

1. All journalists in a district have an equal professional right to send correspondence from that district to any journal or agency, excepting in so far as they are debarred by usage as defined by this Code.

2. It is, as a rule, desirable that correspondents should be chosen from amongst journalists whose ordinary occupation is in the active collection of news or in the preparing of news for the Press.

3. It shall be deemed unprofessional for a journalist to use for correspondence, by linage or otherwise, the copy of another journalist, except as provided by this Code.

4. A journalist (or journalists) who is (or are) recognized by a journal, or agency, as its correspondent (or correspondents) in a district has (or have) an exclusive title to send all correspondence from such district to that journal or agency.

5. A journalist should not send speculative correspondence in ordinary general news to any journal or agency from a district outside his own district, if in such outside district there is in active practice a competent and accredited local correspondent (or correspondents); except *(a)* by arrangement with such local correspondent (or correspondents); or *(b)* in regard to any special and exclusive information.

6. In cases of delegation of duty in the supplying of correspondence, fair remuneration should be given to the journalist who does the work so delegated. Such remuneration should be at the rate of not less than 50 per cent. of the proceeds; and, in the case of salaried correspondents, at such rate as may be mutually agreed upon. It shall be deemed unprofessional for any correspondent to delegate his work, except for temporary and exceptional purposes.

7. A journalist should not accept instructions to supply correspondence, nor send speculative correspondence, on terms below those recognised in his district, defined in case of doubt by meeting of the District of the Institute within which such (correspondence) district is situated.

8. Newspaper proprietors and news agencies should not accept copy from secretaries, members of the public services, coroners, ministers of religion, and other persons in positions of official authority and responsibility, in preference to that of accredited journalists.

9. Nothing in this Code shall be held to prevent any journalist from sending special and exclusive information to any quarter.

It is not always an easy matter to determine whether a reporter who claims to be an accredited correspondent for a particular district is or is not entitled to the designation. To have sent a solitary or an occasional paragraph, and to have had it accepted, is hardly a sufficient justification for the claim; but where the position is once established and recognised, any outside interference with it is regarded as unprofessional. Complaints are made that some reporters, not content with working in their own districts—those covered by their own journals—often trespass upon the preserves of others, and, by deputy or otherwise, extend their operations over an unreasonably large area. These are matters in which it is difficult to legislate with any precision, and they can only be satisfactorily settled by the good sense and brotherly feeling of those concerned. In some instances, reporters are not permitted to do linage on their own account, but are expected to do it in behalf of their editors or proprietors in addition to their regular work. This kind of arrangement is not a very satisfactory one, and is apt to lead to a good deal of soreness, even where the reporter receives extra remuneration for his additional labor. It should, of course, be always understood that, if a reporter is permitted to do outside work on his own account, it should not be allowed to interfere with the due fulfilment of his duties to his regular employer, who has in all cases the first claim upon his services.

Reporters do not usually spend much of their time in teaching shorthand, nor are they always well qualified instructors. Some, however, devote a portion of their spare hours to this occupation, teaching privately or in class, and are thus enabled to make an acceptable addition to their incomes. The teacher should, of course, be thoroughly familiar with the text-books, with the details of which reporters as a rule do not trouble themselves. The best teacher is the one who combines theory with practice. The daily experience of the reporter supplies the one, and he may easily acquire the other by an attentive study of the "*Teacher*" and the "*Manual.*"

CHAPTER XII.

Press Agencies.

NO account of newspaper reporting would be complete that did not comprise some reference to the Press Agencies that have been established chiefly in London for the supply of information to newspapers throughout the country. One of the earliest, if not the earliest of these, was Reuter's Telegraphic Agency, the main object of which was to distribute among the newspapers copies of the telegraphic despatches received from its correspondents in many quarters of the globe. Before the establishment of this office, or company as it is now called, newspapers had to depend for their foreign intelligence upon their own regular correspondents, or occasional contributors. The expense attending this department of journalistic enterprise was too great for any but newspapers of the first rank; but, by providing a common source of supply, the cost was greatly reduced, and brought within the means of almost all the daily and weekly journals of the kingdom. It was some time before the wealthier papers fell in with this arrangement; but, still retaining their special correspondents in the principal capitals of the world, they are all glad to be able to supplement the information received from them by the Reuter despatches, which, for a moderate annual payment, are, as soon as received, forwarded simultaneously to all subscribers. Other telegraphic agencies have since come into the field, and have met with more or less support from the British press. I am not, however, so much concerned with these, which deal mainly with foreign correspondence, as with the ordinary Press Agencies formed for the supply of reports of every kind—meetings, law cases, Parliamentary news, markets, races, and the like—such as come within the scope of the newspaper reporter. I think I may claim the merit of having done a good deal to lead the way to this kind of newspaper work. Soon after settling down in London, in 1849, I saw that there was ample room for such an agency as I have mentioned, and, in conjunction with my two partners, I established a small concern entitled "The Metropolitan Reporting Agency," whose business it was to supply reports of meetings, trials, &c., to country newspapers which had no representatives in London. Many provincial journals found it more convenient to instruct us to send to them reports of matters of local interest taking place in London, than to go to the expense of sending their own reporters to town, perhaps to wait about for many days, say for a trial, the exact date of which could never be relied on with any certainty. The idea was still further developed by others, and nearly every country newspaper now subscribes to one or the other of the Press Agencies from which it receives, according to its necessities, items of general intelligence, together with Parliamentary and other reports, which are forwarded by post, train, or telegraph, as occasion may require. One of the largest of these is the Press Association, Limited, which, in addition to the reports I have mentioned, forwards, by special arrangement with Reuter, the telegrams of that company to the provincial press. For what is called a "full service," the despatch of all telegrams day and night, a charge is made to each country morning paper of £300 per annum; and to each evening paper for day telegrams only £115 per annum; smaller sums being charged for "summaries:" "very short summaries," and "selections," the lowest being £70 a year for morning and £40 for evening papers. There are also special tariffs for commercial news, including reports from the principal Stock Exchanges and Markets; Lloyd's Mail News; Sporting News; General News, and Parliamentary. The cost of a Parliamentary report of from two to two and a half columns per night is £2 10s. per week; if supplemented by special reports of important speeches, £4 4s. per week. A short summary of both Houses during the session is sent for a guinea a week; while the cost of an "express report" for evening papers sent direct from the House of Commons is only fifteen shillings a week. Papers published only once, twice or thrice a week are charged according to the number of days on which the news is supplied. For "special reporting"

—*i.e.* of law cases, meetings, &c.—the charge is eighteen shillings per column, or, if sent to more than one paper, fifteen shillings per column. If forwarded by telegraph, the cost of transmission is equally divided between the newspapers taking the report. These charges are for members only; non-members being charged ten per cent. additional. The Association has a large staff of reporters, most of whom are engaged in Parliament, in the Law Courts, or in both. During the session, some of them are employed in reporting Parliamentary Committees for country papers.

The Central News is another agency of the same character. Its fee for a report of Parliament is £55 for the session, or, if supplemented by full reports of important speeches, £85. Local speeches are charged 18s. per column plus the cost of telegraphing. Reports of law cases, meetings, Parliamentary committees, &c. are supplied on the "linage" principle at 1½d. per line for matter used, with a minimum of 2s., and "at the usual reporting rates, if long reports are ordered."

The Exchange Telegraph Company also transmits news (which it receives through its own private wires from the Gallery, the Law Courts, and elsewhere) to the newspapers. In addition to its General News and Parliamentary Services, it has special services in connection with the Courts of Justice, the Stock Exchange, the markets, and the racecourses. Much of its news is communicated by means of tape machines fixed in the offices of the newspapers, where the messages come direct from their source.

The National Press Agency supplies to country papers stereotyped columns of news and articles of every kind. These are sent daily, if required, by train; and are found extremely convenient and economical, saving the cost of composition and the labor of selection in the country. This Agency also undertakes reporting work at the usual charges.

The Institute of Journalists.

It is only within recent years that the journalists of the United Kingdom have become, like most other professions, an organized body. They now possess an "Institute" which received a royal charter of incorporation in 1890, and now numbers more than two thousand members, of whom a large proportion are reporters for the press. The objects for which the Institute has been established are thus set forth in the charter :—

(*a*) Devising measures for testing the qualifications of candidates for admission to professional membership of the Institute by examination in theory and in practice, or by any other actual and practical tests.
(*b*) The promotion of whatever may tend to the elevation of the status and the improvement of the qualifications of all Members of the Journalistic profession.
(*c*) The ascertainment of the law and practice relating to all things connected with the Journalistic profession, and the exercise of supervision over its members when engaged in professional duties.
(*d*) The collection, collation and publication of information of service or interest to Members of the Journalistic profession.
(*e*) Watching any legislation affecting the discharge by Journalists of their professional duties and endeavouring to obtain amendments of the law affecting Journalists, their duties or interests.
(*f*) Acting as a means of communication between Members or others seeking professional engagements and employers desirous of employing them.
(*g*) Promoting personal and friendly intercourse between Members of the Institute; holding conferences and meetings for the discussion of professional affairs, interests and duties; the compilation, constant revision and publication of lists and registers of Journalists and of records of events and proceedings of interest to Journalists.
(*h*) The formation of a library or libraries for the use Members of the Institute.
(*i*) The encouragement, establishment, or development of a professional journal for journalists.
(*j*) The promotion, encouragement, or assistance of means for providing against the exigencies of age, sickness, death and misfortune.
(*k*) The acquisition by the Institute of a hall or other permanent place of meeting, and of other places of meeting.
(*l*) Securing the advancement of Journalism in all its branches and obtaining for Journalists as such formal and definite professional standing.
(*m*) The promotion by all reasonable means of the interests of Journalists and Journalism.

The Institute consists of five classes, viz., members, fellows, associates, pupil associates, and honorary members. Members must be not less than 21 years of age, and must have been at least two years in actual practice as professional journalists. Fellows are men of recognised professional standing, or of special experience or distinction. Associates are persons ineligible as members or fellows, but, by reason of their relations with journalism, are qualified to concur with journalists in the advancement and service of the profession. Pupil associates must be not less than 16 years of age, and be engaged (under indenture or otherwise) in training for the profession of journalism. Members pay an annual subscription of 10s. 6d.; fellows, £2 2s.; associates, 10s. 6d.; and pupil associates, 5s. A member may compound for future annual subscriptions by a single payment of ten guineas, and a fellow by a single payment of twenty-five guineas. Fellows may use after their names the letters F.J.I., and members, M.J.I. The qualifications recognised by the Institute as constituting any person a journalist within the meaning of the by-laws are

(a) That he is professionally and habitually engaged as Editor of a Journal.
(b) That he is professionally and habitually engaged upon the Staff of a Journal in the capacity of leader-writer, writer of special articles, artist, special correspondent, literary manager, assistant editor, sub-editor, or reporter.
(c) That he is professionally and habitually engaged in supplying journals with articles, illustrations, correspondence or reports.

For the purposes of the Institute, the United Kingdom is divided into districts, each district having its own officers and duties as prescribed by the by-laws.

Among the duties of the Council are

(a) To devise a scheme whereby candidates for admission to the classes of Members, Fellows and Pupil-Associates may prove by examination or other actual and practical test, their professional qualifications for admission.
(b) To encourage, and where possible to initiate, whatever may tend towards improvement of the status, training, and qualification of all classes of Journalists.
(c) To formulate, in so far as may be found desirable, the professional usages and customs of Journalists; and to formulate, protect, and extend where necessary the beneficial privileges of the Press.
(d) To ascertain, for the guidance of members, the state of the law as affecting the conduct of Journalists of their professional duties.
(e) To mediate in regard to, and if possible to reconcile, disputes affecting Members of the Institute.
(f) To collect professional information of every kind for the service of members,

(*g*) To watch all legislative proposals which may affect the efficient and satisfactory conduct of Journalists of their professional duties; and to exert their utmost influence to obtain amendment of such proposals in respect of any matters which may be injurious to the interests and usefulness of the profession.

(*h*) To act as far as may be practicable as a means of intercommunication between members seeking professional engagements and employers desiring to find occupants for vacant posts.

(*i*) To promote to the utmost degree personal and friendly acquaintanceship between members, by the holding of conferences and meetings in all parts of the country for discussion of professional affairs; by the compilation, constant revision, and publication of lists and registers of Journalists, and of records of events and proceedings of interest to Journalists; and by other means.

(*j*) To form a library or libraries for the use of members.

(*k*) To give every encouragement and assistance which may possibly be given, consistently with perfect security to the interests and reputation of the Institute, to the firm establishment or satisfactory development of a professional Journal for Journalists.

(*l*) To devise and propose measures which shall lead towards the adoption by Journalists generally of a scheme or system of providence against the exigencies of age, sickness, death and misfortune; and to aid and encourage in every possible way all endeavours which are made to develop and extend existing systems and organizations established for such objects.

(*m*) To devise measures which shall lead to enhancement of the general standard of remuneration for the professional services of Journalists, especially by means of a previous enhancement of the standard of professional qualification, and by such other sound beneficial means as may be carefully devised.

(*n*) To devise measures which shall lead to the acquisition by the Institute of a Hall or other permanent and sufficient place of meeting; and to aid in the acquisition of permanent and sufficient places of meetings for the several districts, should it be found to be possible and desirable.

The central office of the Institute is 78 Fleet Street, E.C., and the Secretary is Mr. H. Cornish.

CHAPTER XIII.

LONGHAND PRESS CONTRACTIONS.

FOR many years past, a number of what are known as Press contractions have been in use in newspaper offices, especially among the reporters. They greatly diminish the labor of writing, and involve very little difficulty in deciphering on the part of the compositors. They are generally recognised among newspaper printers, and even by the Government Telegraph Offices, whose best operators are employed in transmitting Press messages. Unfortunately, however, there has been a want of uniformity in the use of these abbreviations. This was made the subject of discussion at the International Shorthand Congress in 1887, and a Committee was appointed for the purpose of drawing up a list of contractions most commonly used, in order that it might be distributed among newspaper offices, and, if approved, adopted as a standard. The Committee prepared and published the list agreed upon; but, though no objections have been offered to it, it can hardly be said to have been universally accepted. I now reprint the list, together with the Committee's report, and venture to recommend it for general adoption among Pressmen. Even if it be not the best possible arrangement, it will have the effect of securing uniformity in Press copy, the want of which occasionally leads to error. And I would strongly emphasize the Committee's recommendation as to the importance of writing the contractions with great distinctness, and keeping them well separated from the rest of the MS. The only additional abbreviation that I would suggest is one which I have often used with advantage—the dropping of the letter *e* in words beginning with *ex*, as xpress, xtend, xpire, &c. There can be no possible ambiguity from the elision, and the saving of a letter is worth consideration. The Committee's report is as follows:—

A large proportion of ordinary composition consists, as is well known, of the same words occurring over and over again. For these words reporters habitually use contractions of which literary men have not as yet had the advantage. From comparisons between the quantities of manuscript which can be produced by fast writers with and without reporters' contractions, it would appear that the saving in time thus attainable amounts to from 20 to 30 per cent.

It appears that much inconvenience is caused by the varying and inconsistent contractions of different writers for the Press. One writer, for example, uses a contraction for "the" (t) which another uses for "that;" "fr," which some writers use for "from," is often read and printed as "for;" the "sh," which some use for "shall," is often mistaken for "should;" and longer words, such as "different" and "difficult" (dift), are occasionally confused in the same way. These errors give trouble to authors and printers, and sometimes escape detection altogether until after publication.

Having obtained lists of the contractions in general use in the principal newspaper offices in London and various parts of the country, we found, as might have been expected, that, in spite of occasional discrepancies, there was substantial agreement between them. By carefully collating them, we were able to frame a list which, we believe, comprises the well-known contractions of common words. The list thus compiled was submitted privately to several known printers, literary men, and journalists, and, having received their approbation, was sent to the principal printers in London, with the request that they would hang it up in their printing offices. The reception it has met with entitles us to recommend it as a standard list, and as such we append it to our report.

The list, it will be observed, is confined to contractions of words in general use as distinguished from those which may be considered technical. There are many, for example, which are largely employed in legal documents, such as "exors." and "admors." for "executors" and "administrators," which would not always and everywhere be recognised, and might be mis-printed if found in a totally different connection. Again, most writers make for themselves abbreviations of long words, which they contract more or less according to the frequency of their recurrence in the particular work on which they are engaged; but such abbreviations would not readily explain themselves apart from the subject and context. We have not at present attempted to deal with either of these classes of words.

The list as it stands cannot, we believe, fail to secure to all who use it the two advantages desired, namely, a saving of time and labor in writing and the avoidance of error in printing, provided only that the contractions be distinctly formed, special care being taken that single letters representing words are not joined to others. Any extra care that may at first be required to make the contractions legible, will be far more than compensated for by the saving of time resulting from their use.

(*Signed*) W. H. GURNEY-SALTER (*Chairman*).
G. LESLIE BANNERMAN.
AUGUSTINE BIRRELL.
W. R. GOWERS.
A. R. MARTEN.
T. A. REED.
W. STORR.
THEODORE R. WRIGHT.

Written.	*Printed.*	*Written.*	*Printed.*	*Written.*	*Printed.*
/	the	ab^{t}	about	lge	large
t	that	acc^{t}	account	mt^{g}	meeting
f	for	aft^{n}	afternoon	m^{t}	might
o	of	ag^{n}	again	m^{g}	morning
h	have	agst	against	notw^{g}	notwithstanding
y	you	am^{g}	among	obj^{n}	objection
w	with	am^{t}	amount	o'c	o'clock
r (above the line.)	termination "ver" as how^{r}, which^{r}, when^{r}, wher^{r}	bec	because	op^{n}	opinion
g (above end of verb.)	"ing," as com^{g} lead^{g}	b^{n}	been	opp^{y}	opportunity
n (above the line.)	termination "tion," "sion," or "ion"	btwn	between	o^{r}	other
ce (above the line.)	termination "ance," "ence"	c^{d}	could	o^{t}	ought, alone or as termination, as bro^{t}, brought, tho^{t} thought, &c.
m^{t}	termination "ment"	ch^{n}	chairman	part^{r}	particular
omit 'day' in days of week.	example—"Mon" Monday	cir^{ce}	circumstance	q^{n}	question
		com^{e}	committee	s^{d}	said
		dif^{ce}	difference	sev^{l}	several
		dif^{t}	different	sh	shall
		dif^{ch}	difficult	sh^{d}	should
		dif^{clty}	difficulty	th^{r}	their, there
		xtr^{y}	extraordinary	tho	though
		ev^{g}	evening	thro	through
		evy	every	tog^{r}	together
		f^{m}	from	vy	very
		fu^{r}	further	wh^{r}	whether
		gen	general	w^{h}	which
		gov	government	w^{t}	without
		g^{t}	great	w^{d}	would
		h^{d}	had	yest^{y}	yesterday
		imp^{ce}	importance	y^{r}	your
		imp^{t}	important		

CHAPTER XIV.

CORRECTING PROOFS.

EVERY professional Shorthand writer should have a general acquaintance with the technicalities of the printing office, sufficient, at any rate, to enable him to correct an ordinary printer's "proof." To a journalist this is indispensable. Reporters, it is true, are not always called upon to correct the proofs of their reports; indeed, in many cases, it would be a matter of impossibility, as, for example, in the case of Gallery men, who are often engaged in note-taking while their manuscript, written an hour or two before, is in the printers' hands, and the type "made up" and ready for the press. But in many instances, where time admits, the correction of his proofs is a part of a reporter's duty; to say nothing of cases in which the reporter assists in sub-editing, when other matter than his own comes under his review, not only in manuscript but in the printed "galley" Some reporters are indifferent to these matters, and are content to leave everything to the printer, paying no attention to punctuation, to division into paragraphs, to the use of capitals or italics, and many other little details, the neglect of which indicates carelessness or inexperience, or both. In the case of the professional Shorthand writer, proof-reading is a comparatively rare occupation. In the majority of cases his transcripts are not printed at all; but when, as in important trials, they are put in type day by day, it is not usual to submit the proofs to him for revision. If it were, he would need something more than an iron constitution; since the printing is generally done in the midnight and early morning hours, when, after a hard day's work at note-taking and transcribing or dictating, he naturally expects to be recuperating his energies in sleep and preparing for the next day's toil. But there are occasions on which even he is requested to read and correct the printer's proofs of his transcripts, and he should be able to do it in the orthodox fashion. Indeed, I recommend every shorthand practitioner, even if he is on the lowest rounds of the ladder, to acquire a knowledge of the little details connected with this department of literary labour. It is easily gained, and may sometimes prove of real advantage to the possessor.

Proofs are generally pulled in long slips or galleys, before the type is made up into pages, and a good margin is left on each side for the corrections. When a wrong word or letter appears in the print, it is underlined, and the proper word or letter written opposite in the nearest margin, right or left. This is a very simple matter; but when, as in the case of a "rough proof," corrections have to be made of turned letters, wrong type, mis-spacing, and a host of "literals" that sometimes disfigure the printed page before the printer's reader has had an opportunity of dealing with them, it is almost impossible to correct them satisfactorily without a knowledge of the symbols commonly employed for the purpose. I have therefore had a page "composed" containing most of the typographical errors which meet the eye of a proof-reader, and have shown in the margin the ordinary method of correcting them. To this I have added certain explanations, with a view of rendering the use of the symbols as intelligible as possible. It is, perhaps, hardly necessary to state that underlining a word once in the copy, or in the proof, is an indication to the printer that the word should be printed in italics, and that a double underlining means that it should be printed in capitals.

The Previous Question.[1]

2 The previous question is an ingenious method of 3
4 avoiding a vote upon any question thathas been 5
proposed, but its technical name does little to 6
7 elucidate its operation when there is no de 8
9 bate, or after a debate is closed, the Speaker 10
11 ordinarily puts the question as a matter of course,
without any direction from the House but, by a 12
13 for motion the previous question, the Speakers 14
act may be intercepted and forbidden. 15
The words of this motion are, that the question 16
17 be now put. Those who wish to avoid the 18
19 putting of the ~~chief~~ question ~~main question~~ vote 20
21 against the previous or latter) question, and, if 22
23 it be resolved in the negative, the Speaker is pre
24 vented from puting the main question, as the 25
26 may, how ever, be brought forward again on an- 27
other day; as the negation of the previous 28
29 question merely binds the speaker not to put 30
31 the main *question* at that time. Parliamentary 32
33 Practice.

1. Change from lower case (or small) letters to capitals. For small capitals write "sm. caps."
2. Indent, to show beginning of paragraph.
3. The letter "g" is turned upside down; the symbol in the margin, a small curl, means that the letter is to be re-turned.
4. The letter "v" is wrongly printed in italics; the correction "w f" means "wrong fount."

5. A "space" (a piece of lead used to divide words) has been omitted between the words "that" and "has;" the correction is marked by a caret, as shown, and the mark in the margin.
6. A wrong final letter appears in "does;" the pen is drawn through it, and the right letter is written in the margin. The sloping stroke following the "s" is merely a dividing mark, usually placed after each correction, in case any others should follow in the same line.
7. A comma instead of a full stop is printed after the word "operation;" a circle is drawn round it, and the full stop, encircled, is written in the margin, followed by "W" to show that the next word, "when," must begin with a capital.
8. A hyphen is omitted after "de" at the end of the line; the error is noted by a caret underneath and a hyphen between two vertical or sloping lines in the margin.
9. There is too much space before the word "or;" the sign employed means that the words should be closed up.
10. "Closed" is wrongly printed with a capital "c;" l.c. is an indication that the letter should be "lower case."
11. A full stop is wrongly inserted after the word "question;" the correction is made by a circle in the margin, followed by the letter "d," signifying "dele," the Latin word for "expunge." The letter should be written as shown, and not the ordinary roman or italic "d," which might in some cases be taken to represent that letter itself and not the word "dele."
12. A semicolon is needed after the word "House."
13. The words "for" and "motion" require transposition, and this is indicated by the line drawn as shown and the letters "trs" (transpose) in the margin.
14. An apostrophe is wanted to mark the possessive case in "Speaker's." The sign under the apostrophe in the margin is used to distinguish it from a comma.
15. There should be no new paragraph, but the words should "run on" without a break.
16. The mark between the words "that" and "the" is caused by a "space" standing up; attention may be called to it in several ways, that shown in the margin being perhaps the simplest.
17. A new paragraph (N.P.) should begin with the word "those."
18. Corners of line slipped.
19. Remove the word "chief" and substitute "main."
20. The words "main question" are to be removed, as shown by the letter "d" for "dele."
21. First portion of parenthesis missing before the word "or."
22. The word "question" has been struck through in mistake. The dots underneath mean that it is not to be removed, and "stet" in the margin (meaning "let it stand") is only a confirmation of the instruction to the printer. (When words have been wrongly struck out in MS., if dots are placed under them the compositor will understand that they are to be printed).
23. Bad letter in "*r*esolved." Attention is called to it by a cross.

24. Letter "t" omitted in "puting."
25. Some words have been omitted after "the" at the end of the line. "Out, see copy," is a direction to the printer to refer to the MS. for the missing words, which in the present case are, "House have thus refused to allow it to be put. It."
26. "How ever" to be closed up.
27. Two lines are close together and need to be "leaded" or placed further apart. "Ld" is a contraction for "lead."
28. The words "previous question" should be within quotation marks.
29. Capital instead of small "s."
30. Transpose letters in "ptu."
31. The word "question" to be in roman.
32. "Rule" (or short line) wanted after the word "time."
33. "Parliamentary Practice" to be in italics.

The passage as corrected is as follows:—

THE PREVIOUS QUESTION.

The previous question is an ingenious method of avoiding a vote upon any question that has been proposed, but its technical name does little to elucidate its operation. When there is no debate, or after a debate is closed, the Speaker ordinarily puts the question as a matter of course, without any direction from the House; but, by a motion for the previous question, the Speaker's act may be intercepted and forbidden. The words of this motion are, that the question be now put.

Those who wish to avoid the putting of the main question vote against the previous (or latter) question; and, if it be resolved in the negative, the Speaker is prevented from putting the main question, as the House have thus refused to allow it to be put. It may, however, be brought forward again on another day; as the negation of the "previous question" merely binds the Speaker not to put the main question at that time.—*Parliamentary Practice.*

I have already referred to the importance of accurate punctuation in order to avoid ambiguity or ludicrous misreadings. Actions at law have arisen out of disputed constructions of unpunctuated sentences. It has sometimes been said that good composition should be independent of such aid, and that, if words are properly arranged, they cannot be misunderstood. But the reporter has not always this ideal style of verbal construction to deal with; and cannot therefore afford to dispense with punctuation. If he begins the habit early, he will find it difficult to omit his stops, however rapidly he is turning out his copy; and the printers will be thankful for the assistance thus given to them. There are no absolute rules on the subject. Some punctuate more stiffly than others. I recommend a medium course. In the case of very long sentences it is generally possible, and certainly desirable, to break them up. Young reporters are often afraid of full stops, and never dream of beginning a new sentence with an "And" or a "But," or a "For," even when the sense obviously requires it. The "And" or the "But" or the "For" may have no special reference to the last few words, but rather to the entire sentence that has preceded, or indeed, to several preceding sentences, and to divide the word off by a comma or even a semicolon may be to miss its true significance. If the reporter is conscious that he is weak in the matter of punctuation, or has never given the subject a thought, he should occasionally, when reading a piece of good composition, make a point of studying the use of the stops. He need not follow it in every detail, but it will at least afford him some hints by which he may profit in his own practice.

CHAPTER XV.

Women Reporters.

THERE are departments of Shorthand work for which women are well qualified, and there can be no valid reason why they should not be employed in them. Girls will learn Shorthand as readily as boys, and the lightness and delicacy of touch which belong to their sex, are distinctly favorable to the acquisition of manual dexterity in the use of the Shorthand symbols. It is true that few women, if any, have attained the high speeds acquired by men; but this is probably due to their inferior powers of physical endurance, their inability to go through the amount of labor involved in continuous note-taking which often falls to the lot of the masculine practitioner. And this inability is a disqualification for those branches of reporting in which very long spells at note-taking and transcribing are of common occurrence. I should never recommend a young woman, unless she possessed an exceptionally robust constitution, to undertake reporting engagements that might necessitate the sitting for many hours in a crowded hall or court, and then spending many more hours in the night or early morning in the work of transcribing, often exposing herself to sudden changes of temperature and vicissitudes of weather which are trying to the strongest frames. Nor would I advise any young lady of my acquaintance to attempt law reporting, which, in addition to the objectionable feature I have mentioned, often presents aspects from which almost any woman of delicate sensibilities would shrink with pain, if not with disgust. But apart from these fields of labor, there are many spheres of usefulness which a well trained and intelligent young woman may well occupy with advantage to herself and others. As an amanuensis, for either literary or commercial purposes, she is admirably qualified. In the Post Office and other departments of the public service women have proved their efficiency for clerical work; and Shorthand opens to them another door to remunerative occupation. I can see no objection to their reporting public meetings (except under the unfavorable circumstances to which I have alluded), lectures, sermons, and many other functions in which they may utilize their shorthand acquirements. Every young woman, however, who desires to make the most of her shorthand, should also learn to use the typewriter—another occupation in which her supple fingers (which have probably had some similar training on the piano), should render her at least as expert as the other sex. With the two accomplishments combined, a well educated woman should have no difficulty in finding suitable employment. Many have already entered the field; and a few ladies are to be seen occasionally at the reporters' table at public meetings. They have not yet found their way to the Reporters' Gallery in the Houses of Parliament; but efforts have been made even in that direction. Nor have they, except in one or two instances, and then only for a few days or weeks, appeared in the Law Courts either as newspaper reporters or as shorthand writers. I believe that in America women have even been appointed as official shorthand writers in some of the courts, while others have a good private practice as "stenographers"—the term generally employed in the States. Employment of this kind is of course, to a great extent, incompatible with domestic life, and has often to be abandoned for home duties of an imperative description. But this is an obstacle to almost all departments of out-of-door labor undertaken by women, and will probably always prevent their attaining so high a degree of efficiency or of professional eminence as that achieved by their male competitors who are not thus handicapped in the race.

CHAPTER XVI.

TELEGRAPHING.

SO much of the reporter's work is in these days transmitted by telegraph that I should hardly be excused if I omitted to say something in regard to this marvellous agency. Within the memory of many living persons a telegraphic despatch, however brief, was regarded as little short of a miracle; and even after the introduction of the now familiar "wire," it was some years before it was utilized to any considerable extent for press purposes. Short messages of a few words or lines were despatched on rare occasions to the principal newspapers. The method of transmission was slow and cumbrous; and a message of a few hundred words was almost unheard of. But the development of telegraphy has been no less striking than that of stenography. With the growing demand for rapid communication, there have come successive improvements in the machines employed, till it is now possible, by a suitable division of labor among the operators, to transmit by wire an average of 250 words per minute, so that the longest speech delivered in the evening in the remotest part of the kingdom, can be sent to London and all the chief centres of population in time for publication in the journals of the following morning. That this is a matter of almost daily occurrence in the busy season, every newspaper reader can testify. Reporters who have frequently to use the telegraph for press messages should make themselves familiar with the Post Office regulations on the subject, a neglect of which may lead to delay and disappointment. I append a copy of the latest circular issued by the Post Office, which contains full details for the guidance of pressmen, including a tariff of charges:—

PRESS MESSAGES.

CHARGES.

The rates for the transmission of press messages are as follows:—

1*s.* for every 100 words, or fraction of 100 words, between 6 p.m. and 9 a.m.; and 1*s.* for every 75 words, or fraction of 75 words, between 9 a.m. and 6 p.m.

When a message is sent to more than one address, *2d.* for every 100 or 75 words, as the case may be, sent to each additional address.

The addresses need not be in the same town.

A message, if handed in at 9 a.m. precisely, will be charged at the day rate, and if handed in at 6 p.m. precisely, at the night rate.

The names and addresses of the senders and addressees of press telegrams are not counted or charged for.

Figures are counted and charged for at the rate of one word for each figure.

If the receiver of a press message doubts the accuracy of any portion of it, he may have the doubtful portion repeated on depositing the sum of *6d.* for each 100 or 75 words, according to the time of night or day at which the application for a repetition is made. In the event of any error having been made in transmission, the money will be refunded.

CONDITIONS.

A press message must be addressed to public newspapers or institutions which have been registered at the General Post Office.

It must be addressed to a newspaper at its registered address; if addressed to the editor, publisher, or other member of the staff by name, it will be liable to be charged at the full rate for ordinary messages. It must contain matter solely for publication in the newspaper to which it is addressed.

Telegrams sent to a newspaper, but not intended for immediate publication in that newspaper, are chargeable at the full rate for ordinary messages.

Telegrams sent to newspapers at the press rates must not be exhibited at the newspaper offices for public inspection.

The Postmaster General will not be liable for any loss or damage which may be incurred or sustained by reason, or on account, of any mistake or default in the transmission or delivery of a telegram.

WHAT A PRESS MESSAGE MAY NOT CONTAIN.

A press message may not contain :—

(1). Letters to the editor.

(2). Advertisements.

(3). Ordinary notices of births and deaths.

(4). Election addresses.

(5). Anything not intended for immediate publication in the newspaper, or immediate exhibition in the news room, club, or exchange room, to which it is addressed.

(6). Anything written in cypher or in a foreign language.

(7). Anything for the publication of which a money payment is usually made.

When any such matter, or matter of a private nature, or matter not for publication, is included in or added to a press message, such matter will be charged for at the full rate for ordinary messages. For instance, the words "To follow report sent by train," if prefixed to a press message, are chargeable as a separate message at the full rate.

An exception to the foregoing rule is made in the case of the following "instructions," which, being intended for the guidance of the officers of the Department, are permitted to be transmitted free of charge:—

"More to follow."—When written at the end of a section of a message which is being handed in in sections.

"Continuation of—message."—When written at the commencement of a section.

"End of Message."—When written at the conclusion of a message.

These words will not be counted with, or charged for as, a portion of the message.

PREPAYMENT.

The charge for the transmission and the charge, (if any) for the delivery of a press message must be paid at the time of tender, except in the case of any message to which a pass is attached entitling the message to be accepted for transmission without prepayment.

PASSES.

Proprietors of newspapers, whether London or provincial, will be provided by the Department with books containing passes for the transmission of press messages without prepayment on the following conditions:—

i. A minimum deposit of 25*l*. to be lodged with the Postmaster-General, to cover the value of the franked messages and as security for the credit given.

ii. The accounts for the messages sent under the passes—which will be rendered by the Receiver and Accountant General monthly—to be paid within one week of the date on which they are received.

iii. A charge of 2½ per cent. to be paid on the amount of each account, to meet the expense incurred in keeping an account of the messages sent, and to defray the cost of printing the passes.

iv. The passes to be used only for the purpose of franking messages addressed to the newspaper, the name of which is printed thereon. This rule does not apply to the special passes issued to the News Agencies, which frank messages addressed to any newspapers.

Passes which have been defaced or altered in any way will not be accepted.

When one address (or more) in a "multiple-address" message is franked by a pass, and the remaining addresses are paid for in stamps, one of these latter addresses must be paid for at the full day or night rate, as the case may be.

METHOD OF WRITING OUT PRESS MESSAGES.

The pages should be numbered consecutively at the right hand top corner; the name of the sender should be written at the top of each page.

Each page should contain about 100 words, and the last word of each page should be repeated at the top of the next.

When more than one reporter is employed on the same message, it should be divided into sections, as A, B, C, &c.; the section letter and page number should be entered at the top of each sheet, and the words "end of section—" at the bottom of the last sheet of each section.

Attention is specially directed to the necessity of writing as legibly as possible, and it is recommended that whenever practicable the "copy" should be written in ink and not in pencil.

When a message is addressed to more than one town, a sufficient number of copies of the text must be supplied to allow of its being telegraphed simultaneously to each town. Information as to the number required can always be obtained beforehand from the postmaster of the town from which the news is sent.

"CONTINUOUS" MESSAGES.

The rules with regard to "continuous" messages, *i.e.*, messages which are handed in in several portions, are as follows:—

i. The whole message must relate to one matter (as, for example, a report of a speech or meeting) complete in itself, and must necessarily be printed consecutively in order to render it intelligible.
ii. It must be sent to one set of addresses.
iii. No portion of copy tendered for transmission between 9 a.m. and 6 p.m. can be counted together with a portion tendered between 6 p.m. and 9 a.m.
iv. No portion of copy handed in must consist of less than 75 words between the hours of 9 a.m. and 6 p.m., or of less than 100 words between the hours of 6 p.m. and 9 a.m. When any batch contains less than these numbers it is charged for as if containing them.
v. In the case of reports of speeches, the "copy" must be tendered consecutively at intervals sufficiently short to keep the telegraphists fully occupied, but not in less quantities than 75 or 100 words at a time (see par. iv.); and in the case of other messages the interval between the handing in of the different batches must not be greater than one hour between the hours of 6 p.m. and 9 a.m., and half-an-hour between the hours of 9 a.m. and 6 p.m.
vi. In any case, should the authorised interval be exceeded, a fresh charge will be calculated from the commencement of the portion next following the break.

NOTICE OF INTENDED DESPATCH OF PRESS MESSAGES.

At least 24 hours' previous notice, by letter or paid telegram, should be given to "The Secretary, General Post Office, London," of the intention to send a press message of a greater length than 200 words.

The notice should contain the following particulars:—

1. Name of Office at which the message will be handed in
2. Time of handing in.
3. Length.
4. Addresses.

In the absence of such notice a press message exceeding 200 words in length cannot be accepted for transmission unless it be considered probable by the postmaster that it can be transmitted in due course without seriously delaying the transmission of ordinary postal telegrams.

When notice has been given that special facilities will be required for the transmission of a press message containing more than 200 words, and it is subsequently found impossible or undesirable to send the message at the time specified, immediate notice should be given to the Secretary by letter or paid telegram during the day; or if the determination not to send the message should be arrived at after 4 p.m., to the postmaster of the office at which the news will be handed in. Otherwise the person giving the notice will be called upon to defray the expense incurred in making arrangements for the work.

Exception.—At the Central Office in London, and the offices in Fleet Street, the Strand, and the House of Commons, messages containing less than 1,000 words can be accepted without notice if addressed to newspapers in the more important provincial towns.

SPECIAL ARRANGEMENTS.

If practicable, without undue expense and without inconvenience to the public service, special arrangements will be made (without late fees) for keeping any telegraph office open after the ordinary business hours for the acceptance, transmission, or delivery of a press message *exceeding* 500 *words in length.* This can only be done when at least 24 hours' notice has been given to the Secretary, General Post Office, by letter or paid telegram, naming the office at which the message is to be tendered, and the addresses at which it is to be delivered, and stating with all practicable accuracy its probable length, and the time at which it will probably be tendered for transmission.

LATE FEES.

In cases not provided for by the last preceding Regulation, postmasters are at liberty to keep their offices open for the acceptance of press messages after the ordinary business hours, and for the transmission of such messages to any Postal Telegraphic Office which is open at the time, or the attention of which (if the office is closed) can be gained, and the postmaster of each office so kept open is authorised to accept (in addition to the ordinary press message charge) and to retain for his own use and for the use of his clerks the following fees by way of remuneration for such special service:—

(1). For each message not exceeding 500 words in length, irrespective of the number of newspapers to which it may be addressed—

(*a*). If the office is open for ordinary postal business, but not for telegraph work, 1*s.* for the clerk and 6*d.* for a messenger if one be required to call the clerk.

(*b*). If the office is open for the receipt by wire of press messages, but not for other ordinary telegraphic work, 6*d.* for the postmaster and 6*d.* for the clerk.

(*c*). If the office is not open for either postal or telegraph work, 1*s.* for the postmaster and 1s. for the clerk.

(2). For each message exceeding 500 words the like fees for each 500 words, and also for any additional fraction of 500 words.

(3). For each continuous message, part of which was tendered for transmission during ordinary business hours, the like fees for so much of the message as is tendered for transmission after ordinary business hours.

(4). When several press messages are tendered by the same person and at one time, such messages are to be counted together and dealt with as a single message for all the purposes of this Regulation.

(5). Separate fees are payable under this Regulation by each person who tenders a telegram for transmission out of ordinary business hours.

(6). If notice has been given requesting an office to be kept open for the acceptance of a press message at a specified time out of ordinary business hours, and the message is not in fact tendered for more than one hour after the specified time, a postmaster is authorised to receive a second set of fees for such messages under this Regulation.

(7). All fees payable under this Regulation shall be paid by the sender of the message to the postmaster or other officer to whom it is tendered for transmission, and shall be retained or paid over to him, as the case may be, to the person or persons entitled to receive the same under this Regulation.

SPECIAL WIRES.

When the number of wires will permit of it, the Postmaster-General will be willing to grant to a newspaper the use of a special wire, from the telegraph office in one town to the telegraph office in another town, for an annual rental of 500*l.*, payable quarterly, the wire to be worked for six nights in each week, commencing at 6 p.m. each night.

The Post Office will provide the apparatus, telegraphists, &c. necessary for the proper working of the wire, and will deliver the messages at the office of the newspaper free of cost, provided the distance does not exceed half a mile from the terminal Postal Telegraph Office. The special wire can, if desired, be extended to the offices of the newspaper at either end; but for the lengths of the wire connecting the newspaper offices with the telegraph offices a fixed annual rental, on the scale laid down in the Post Office Guide will be charged in addition to the rental of 500*l.* The news transmitted over the wire must be used solely for publication in the newspaper for the service of which it is rented.

It will be seen from the circular that the Post Office offers every accommodation to the representatives of the press. Whenever a reporter is engaged in a distant town from which he has to wire copy to his journal, his first care should be to see that proper notice is given at the telegraph office, and to give the necessary information as to when his first copy will be ready, what instalments will follow, and what the entire length of his report is likely to be. Attention to these details will greatly facilitate the transmission. Of course it is not always possible to give accurate information beforehand. The length of a report may depend on circumstances not known at the time of the notice; and there may be some uncertainty as to the time at which a message may be ready. The Post Office is always ready to make allowance for these contingencies; but every effort should be made to keep it adequately informed as to the services that will be required of it, in order that it may make the necessary arrangements for transmission. I may mention that the ordinary press contractions may always be used in sending press messages.

CHAPTER XVII.

Parliamentary Reporting.

As the young barrister, on entering professional life, is said to direct his gaze to the Woolsack, and the private soldier to dream of the Marshal's bâton that the great Emperor declared was in his knapsack, so the young reporter finds the goal of his ambition in the "Gallery," the familiar designation of the rows of seats appropriated to the Press in Parliament. To the more aspiring, however, this position of "airy supremacy," as someone has called it, is but the stepping stone which they fondly hope will conduct them to fame and distinction in other walks of life—law, politics, or literature—which gallery men have often achieved, and to which their journalistic experience within the walls of St. Stephen's has largely contributed. The examples of Campbell and Dickens and Collyer, and of many a Parliamentary celebrity who has won his way from the Gallery to the floor of the House, naturally inspire the youthful reporter who is endowed with energy and talent, with the desire to follow in their footsteps and win the same rewards. The employment is one which is certainly full of interest; and, if intelligently pursued, should train the mind for other and higher work. A better introduction to politicial life can hardly be imagined. But I am not here concerned so much with the ultimate destinies of the occupants of the Gallery, as with their actual work when engaged in chronicling the sayings and doings of our legislators. Nor is it necessary that I should dwell at length upon the history of Parliamentary reporting from the days when it was carried on by stealth, and at the peril of the pillory or the prison, to our own times, when the words of our senators are uttered in the hearing of the multitude, and their actions performed in almost as fierce a light as that which "beats upon a throne." Every daily newspaper in the country devotes a portion of its space to the record of parliamentary proceedings, which is supplied either by its own reporters or by one of the press agencies in London. Each of the London morning dailies has a corps of reporters of its own in the Gallery, and some of the evening papers have representatives in attendance during the early hours of the evening up to the time of issue of their latest editions. The *Times'* corps is the largest, and its report is accordingly fuller than that of any of the other journals, often extending to as many pages as the others occupy columns. No absolutely verbatim report of the debates is published. Even the *Times'* report is more or less condensed, except in the case of speeches of the first importance, while the reports of some of the other journals are little more than the briefest summaries of the principal speeches and a bare mention of the rest. The official report itself, the "Hansard" of former days, now Reuter's Debates, is to some extent abridged, especially in the House of Commons, but it is, perhaps, the most complete record obtainable of Parliamentary proceedings. Excellent reports appear in a few of the best provincial dailies, sometimes indeed, although transmitted by telegraph, exceeding in length those that appear in the metropolitan journals. The result is that in every corner of the empire where a newspaper circulates, the sayings and doings of Parliament are made known with a substantial accuracy and a completeness that scarcely leave anything to be desired.

The work of the Gallery Reporter is of a very responsible character, and, as a rule, only experienced hands are engaged in it. It is not that the speeches are particularly rapid or difficult. There are fast speakers in the House, but the majority of them are fairly deliberate. The chief difficulty is that of hearing. The reporters are at a considerable distance from the speakers, and if the latter are not very distinct in their utterances, there is little chance of their words reaching the Gallery in such a way as to be heard and recorded with any degree of certainty. In the case of inferior speakers this is of no serious moment; but if a minister, or a leading member of the Opposition, is making a statement of great national and political importance, every word of which will be eagerly scanned not only at home but abroad, the reporter has to strain every nerve to catch each syllable as it is uttered, and is often sorely perplexed in the effort to supply expressions that have escaped even the trained and cultured ear of a professional listener. The difficulty of an inexperienced hand engaged in work of this description will be easily understood.

The reporter should not only be a good note-taker, but should be *au courant* with current political events and familiar with the forms and modes of procedure of the House. It is true that except on the staff of the *Times* and one or two other journals there is but rare occasion for the exercise of any great stenographic skill; but now and then, even in a greatly abridged report, the necessity will arise for a strictly verbatim rendering of some phrase or sentence of special interest or importance, and the reporter who is not equal to the task may have to regret his temerity in undertaking it. A knowledge of the forms of procedure may, of course, be soon acquired by experience and observation; but they are a source of some perplexity to the beginner.

It is generally known that most of the Gallery work is done by a system of relays, or "turns." This is necessitated by the imperious demands for a rapid and continuous supply of copy for the printers. The tendency is to make the turns shorter and shorter. If a reporter had to take notes say for an hour, he would need four or five or six hours for his transcription, and his paper might be required to go to press long before it could be completed. By means of short turns of a quarter of an hour, all hands are soon at work, and the notes can be transcribed without loss of time. Each paper has its own arrangements to meet its special requirements, but there is a general resemblance among them all. On the *Times* the turns are a quarter of an hour till eleven o'clock, when they are shortened to ten minutes or less.

There have, of late years, been some changes in the hours of meeting of the two Chambers. Formerly the Lords met at five o'clock, the idea being that the business could be got through by dinner-time. Some of the younger peers complained that they were deterred from initiating debates lest they should trench upon the dinner hour; and, to give them the opportunity they desired of taking a more active part in the proceedings, the hour of meeting was altered to four, public business beginning at half-past. It is a very rare occurrence for debates in the Lords to extend beyond eight o'clock. The Commons at one time met at four o'clock on Monday, Tuesday,

Thursday and Friday, and rose in the early morning hours. On Wednesdays it has long been accustomed to meet at noon and adjourn at six. It now meets at three on Mondays, Tuesdays, Thursdays and Fridays, except when there are what are called morning sittings, when it meets at two. There is on these days an adjournment at seven o'clock for dinner, the House resuming at nine. When there is nothing exceptional on the paper, opposed business stops at midnight. From ten to twenty minutes are then spent in going through the "orders," and the House adjourns. It occasionally happens that there is a long conversation on a bill, or on a motion, without any formal opposition; and in such a case it may be continued; but at one o'clock everything is brought to an abrupt termination by the Speaker leaving the chair. The knowledge that no debate can arise after twelve or one o'clock is a great boon to the reporters, who, instead of having to wait till the House rises, can often leave at an earlier period, according to their position on the rota, with the certainty that they will not be called upon for another turn.

When the House meets at three, and private business is taken, the first turn on the *Times* is half an hour. This period (except towards the end of the Session) is generally occupied with business of a formal character which needs very little attention on the part of the reporter, viz., the presentation of petitions, and the advancement of private bills relating to railways and other local enterprises. "Question time," however, makes an imperative demand upon the reporters' energies; and then the turns are a quarter of an hour. The questions themselves give no trouble since they are printed in the daily "Votes." The answers by the ministers to whom they are addressed, and the lively conversations which sometimes follow them, need the most careful attention. Some ministers are considerate enough to send copies of their answers to the gallery; but where this is not done, and where the question is one of great political importance, it is essential that a very accurate note should be taken of the reply, which is sure to be eagerly read throughout the country, and possibly throughout the world. When the questions, which may occupy an hour, have been disposed of, the regular debates begin and continue throughout the evening, with a brief adjournment during the dinner hour. The important speakers generally manage to speak early or late in the evening, avoiding the hours from eight to ten when the House is almost empty, and when only the second and third-rate speakers are heard. It is during this interval that the reporters have their lightest work, the merest summaries of the speeches being required for the papers. Public business begins at a quarter-past three, and the first turn is then a quarter of an hour. At twelve or one o'clock most of the reporters retire, leaving a few of their colleagues, who are known as "victims," to complete the work. The victim period of the *Times* begins at one o'clock, and two, or three, or four are left, according to the character of the business and the expected length of the sitting. On some of the other papers, a single victim suffices for the closing hours, and his brief report is "written up" in longhand as the debate continues.

The Gallery reporters of to-day look back with some regret on the Wednesdays of the past, when the debates were very briefly reported, and only half the usual corps was required to be in attendance, the other half indulging in a holiday, unless their assistance was needed in reporting some important speech at a dinner or other public function. Wednesday was, and still is, a favourite day for such gatherings, Members of Parliament being then liberated from their evening sittings, and able to attend. Most of these dinner speeches and political meetings are reported by members of the Parliamentary staff. Indeed, on other days than Wednesdays, Gallery men are taken out for such events, and the staff at the House is sometimes unduly depleted.

Most of the morning papers have private wires, through which communication can, when necessary, be made with the Gallery. The *Times*, a few years since, tried the experiment, when the House sat very late, of transmitting its reports by telephone; a reader of the reporter's MS. dictating from the House directly to the compositor in Printing House Square. The experiment was not successful, and it is not, I think, likely to be repeated.

It is usual for a Gallery reporter to be at his post, or within call, some little time before his turn begins, in order to provide for the contingency of his predecessor being, from illness or any other cause, unable to attend. If, however, it is known that all the men on the list are present and ready for work, this precaution is not necessary. It sometimes happens, indeed, that a reporter requires the whole of the interval between one turn and another to complete his transcript, having no margin to spare for the purpose I have mentioned. It is always desirable to be in attendance at least a few minutes before the turn begins, in order to get some idea of the business immediately before the House, or to catch the drift of a speaker's line of argument before beginning to take notes.

The number of reporters employed in the Gallery has greatly increased during the last twenty years. The following is the number of Press tickets issued to the different newspapers and agencies:—

Aberdeen Journal 1; *Belfast News Letter* 1; *Bradford Observer* 1, and 1 leader-writer; *Bristol Times and Mirror* 1; Central News 10; Central Press 4; *Cork Examiner* 1; *Daily Chronicle* 8, and 1 leader-writer; *Daily News* 11, and 1 leader-writer; *Daily Telegraph* 12, and 1 leader-writer; *Dublin Daily Press* 2, and 1 leader-writer; *Dundee Advertiser* 1; *Aberdeen Free Press* 1; *Scottish Leader* 2; *Dundee Courier* 2; *Eastern Morning News* 2; *Evening News* 1; Exchange Telegraph Co. 1, and 1 leader-writer; *Echo* 1; *Freeman's Journal* 6; *Belfast Morning News* 1; *Glasgow Daily Mail*, 5; *Glasgow Herald* 6, and 1 leader-writer; *Globe* 5, and 1 leader-writer; *Graphic* 1 (Thursdays only); Reuter's (Hansard's) Official Corps 10; *Irish Daily Independent* 1; *Irish Times* 3, and 1 leader-writer; *Illustrated London News* 1 (one day only); *Irish Nationalist Press* 1; *Lancet* 1 leader-writer (Monday only); *Leeds Mercury* 2; *Liverpool Daily Post* 1; *Liverpool Courier* 2; *Lloyd's Weekly News* 1 leader-writer (two nights weekly); *Manchester Guardian* 2; *Manchester Courier* 3; *Moonshine* 1; *Morning Advertiser* 9; *Morning Post* 11, and 1 leader-writer and 1 editor; National Press Agency 1; *Newcastle Daily Chronicle* 2; *Northern Whig* 1; *Pall Mall Gazette* 2, and 1 leader-writer; Press Agency 2; Press Association 14, and 1 leader-writer; *Punch*, the Editor (Tuesday's only); Reuter's Telegraph Co. 4; *Scotsman* 6, and 1 leader-writer; *Spectator* 1 (one day only); *Standard* 13, and 1 leader-writer; *St. James's Gazette* 1, and 1 leader-writer; *Times* 16, and 1 leader-writer; *Truth*, the Editor; *Western Daily Mercury* 2; *Western Morning News* 4; *Yorkshire Post* 1. The numbers above given include the summary-writers and chiefs of corps. The leader-writers' tickets are transferable; the others are non-transferable, and bear the names of the holders.

The accommodation for transcribing notes within the precincts of the House, which was formerly very restricted, has of late been greatly extended. It was for many years limited to a few dingy and stuffy ante-rooms just outside the Gallery; and, when these were found to be insufficient for the increasing numbers yearly pouring into it, a large Committee Room (No. 18) was placed at the service of the Press representatives. But even this was inadequate to meet the growing demands, and some of the apartments of a deceased official were appropriated to the Gallery, thus affording a large amount of additional accommodation, including a smoking and reading room, and a small room specially allotted to the *Times*.

Greatly improved arrangements have also been made for providing refreshments to the Gallery corps. Within the recollection of some of the older members, the arrangements were of a very primitive character. The reporters could, if they pleased, dine in the "Strangers'" Refreshment Room in the basement of the building. The only other refreshment obtainable was that provided by the doorkeeper, who, in a small passage—it could hardly be designated a room—served out cups of tea, eggs, bread and butter, and slices of ham or beef, brought from his own house. The reporters have now the advantage of a dining and a tea room. The provisions were until recently supplied from the Members' Dining Room, by a special arrangement between the Gallery Committee and the House of Commons Kitchen Committee. They are now supplied by the Army and Navy Co-operative Association in Westminster, and the arrangement, I believe, gives general satisfaction.

In the new large writing room, a reference library has been provided. Some of the books have been presented by past and present members of the Gallery, the chief donor being Mr. Macintyre, of the *Daily Telegraph*; others have been bought by the Gallery Committee out of funds arising from a subscription of 2s. 6d., levied upon each holder of a Gallery ticket for the Session. Newspapers and reviews are provided for the tea-room and the smoke-room. In the tea-room, there is also a small lending library, consisting of books which have been presented. A set of Parliamentary papers is provided by the House for the use of the Gallery. These are kept in the large writing-room under the care of an attendant.

The Gallery, itself, is situated immediately over the Speaker's chair, extending the whole width of the House, and having a double row of seats. This was, for many years, found sufficient for all ordinary purposes; but, when the provincial press and the news agencies put in their claims for representation—claims that could not long be resisted—it became essential that further accommodation should be supplied. For this purpose, portions of the Members' Galleries, running along the two sides of the house, were added to the Reporters' Gallery, thus affording five additional front seats and six additional back seats. The total number of front seats, or "boxes," including those at the side, is now twenty-nine, and of back seats (which are not spaced off), about thirty-six. In addition to these, there is supposed to be standing room to accommodate (if such a word can be employed,) some twenty persons, who may be in waiting to take their turns, or even engaged in note-taking when no sitting room is available. The front seats are the only ones really suitable for taking notes. The back seats were originally intended for reporters waiting to relieve their colleagues; but they have long since been utilized in meeting the clamorous demands for admission from country papers, "London Letter" writers, leader-writers, and others, who, as press representatives, consider themselves entitled to accommodation. The result is, that the Gallery is greatly crowded, and the continual passing to and fro for the interchange of seats and other purposes, is very inconvenient, and adds to the difficulty of hearing the speakers below.

The three middle front seats are appropriated to the *Times*, one for the chief of the corps, one for the note-taker, and one for the summary writer. The other morning papers have each two front seats, one for the reporter in attendance, and one for the summary-writer; two others are assigned to the Press

Association and the same number to the Central News. Of the extra boxes on the left side, one is appropriated to the *Scotsman* and another to the *Glasgow Herald*, the others being used by certain combinations. On the other side, one of the front seats is occupied by the Dublin *Freeman's Journal.* These side seats are not without their special advantages. They are almost immediately over the Ministerial bench and the Opposition bench respectively. The *Scotman's* is the best for hearing the ministers; and the reporter occupying that seat often catches a word or a sentence in a Ministerial reply which has altogether escaped the other note-takers.

In the House of Lords' Gallery there are only twelve front seats, which are assigned to the London dailies, and fourteen back seats which are mainly occupied by the Press Agencies and the specially favored provincial papers. The acoustic properties of the Upper Chamber are even worse than those of the Lower; and grievous complaints have been made from time to time of the imperfect reports given of their lordships' speeches. The peers themselves have complained of being misrepresented; and the reporters of being unable to hear what is said, and therefore, to present a satisfactory report. Attempts have been made to improve the accommodation, but, except in the case of the official reporter referred to elsewhere, nothing has been done in this direction.

As already mentioned, the *Times* Parliamentary reports are much fuller than those of any other newspaper. The *Standard* was for some years a formidable rival in this respect, but, like all the other morning papers, it is now greatly distanced by the leading journal. Even the *Times*, however, until quite recently, did not hesitate to "keep down" the debates in order to make room for other intelligence of an important character. For several years past it has made a great effort to report the speeches very fully (not always verbatim), and it now issues the debates in a weekly publication, competing with the official reports at a lower price.

At the beginning of the week a rota is prepared by the chief of each corps indicating the order in which the members are expected to be in attendance. The first reporter in the Commons one week is usually the first in the Lords in the following week, and the positions are shifted on from time to time.

CHAPTER XVIII.

Official Parliamentary Reporting.

It is not a little strange that the British Houses of Parliament should be without official reporters of its own, and should have had for so many years to depend upon the records made by private enterprise. Many other nations have their own parliamentary stenographic corps, receiving stipulated salaries, and being regarded as State servants, with all the privileges appertaining to their official position. The British Parliament has been content to rely on a subsidized publication over which it has exercised no control, and for which, therefore, it had no responsibility.

For many years "Hansard" was recognised as a *quasi*-official report of parliamentary proceedings, and was continually cited as a more or less authoritative record of speeches in both Houses. It is a continuation of the "Parliamentary History," which is a selection and compilation of all the records of Parliament from 1066 to 1803. The two publications comprise no fewer than 450 volumes, and contain a continuous record of our parliamentary proceedings from the Conquest to the present day. Down to 1857 the volumes were produced entirely at private expense, being supported only by private subscriptions, the Government contributing nothing to the cost of the preparation of the work. About that time a slight amount of official support was given to the undertaking, the Treasury subscribing for a hundred (afterwards increased to 120) copies for distribution among the public departments and in the colonies. At that time the sessional subscription was fixed at five guineas.

So matters went on for about twenty years, but not without some complaints being made as to the character of the reporting. Nor is this surprising, considering the manner in which the reports were prepared. For a long time it was imagined that "Hansard" had a reporting staff of its (or his) own, and even members of Parliament themselves were not exactly aware of the *modus operandi* pursued. The reports were almost entirely collated from the newspapers, chiefly from the *Times*, and, when printed, were submitted in proof to the speakers, who, if they were so disposed, revised them before they were published. Now and then a speaker would write out his own speech and forward it to "Hansard" for publication. With this exception, the publishers were altogether dependent upon the London papers for the reports, and as these were very often considerably condensed, especially in the case of very long or uninteresting debates, the official report was necessarily imperfect. This imperfection was mainly noticeable in regard to (1) discussions on private bills, (2) debates in committee on public bills, when the clauses were taken into consideration, (3) debates in committee of supply, sometimes involving minute matters of account, and (4) debates after midnight when, however important the subject of discussion might be, the newspapers were unable to report it fully, the hour of going to press being close at hand. The complaints as to these reports increased till at length, in 1867, the then Chancellor of the Exchequer, Sir Stafford Northcote, took the subject into serious consideration, and the result was an agreement with Mr. Hansard whereby he undertook, in consideration of a grant of £3,000, to report more fully the debates on the four points above mentioned. In order to carry out this arrangement, it was of course necessary that a special staff of reporters should be engaged—not a large one, but a small staff able to cope with the proceedings under the four specified heads. The other portion of the debates was to be dealt with as before, namely, by taking them from the fullest and best reports appearing in the daily London or provincial press. I include the provincial press, because at that time country papers of established position were getting into the habit of reporting parliamentary proceedings at great length, especially the speeches of local members, which were often more fully given in the papers published in the town they represented than in the London papers. In some instances, indeed, the members themselves either wrote their speeches for their constituents, or had them specially reported and forwarded to the country papers for publication. Thus the provincial journals were laid under contribution by "Hansard," with great advantage, in the compilation of the semi-official report.

The new arrangement, though regarded as a great improvement upon the old one, did not give entire satisfaction, and some of the Members of Parliament began to clamour for a full official report of Parliamentary debates in the true sense of the term. Mr. Hanbury Tracy (Lord Sudeley) moved in the House of Commons for the appointment of a Select Committee "to consider the expediency of providing official reports of the debates in this House." There was a long debate upon the subject, in which the advantages of a complete record of parliamentary speeches were strongly enforced; but the motion was in the end negatived by a majority of 24. Shortly afterwards, however, in 1878, a Select Committee was appointed to consider the general subject of Parliamentary reporting. It held many sittings, and received the evidence of many Members of Parliament, Parliamentary officials, and gentlemen connected with the newspaper press. One of the main topics discussed before the Committee was the expediency of providing full or verbatim reports of all speeches in Parliament, as to which there were, as there still are, great diversities of opinion. Complaints were made of "Hansard," not only for its imperfect reports, but for the great delay in their publication; but not a few of the witnesses stoutly maintained that it would be undesirable to reproduce and perpetuate all the small talk in which Members of Parliament might choose to indulge, and that "Hansard" satisfied all reasonable requirements. The Committee ultimately reported in favour of the continuance of the arrangement with "Hansard," but added that they were of opinion "that Mr. Hansard should make provision for a more prompt publication of the debates, even at some additional charge upon the votes, if it should appear that the present contribution is not sufficient for the purpose." A similar inquiry was held in 1880 by the House of Lords, a Committee of which reported in favour of the "Hansard" system with some slight expansion. It was accordingly continued, but owing to the great and increasing length of the debates, Mr. Hansard "struck" for an increased allowance, and was fortunate enough to get the Treasury to listen to his appeal. In one Session, that of 1882, the reports extended to no fewer than ten volumes. Taking this and other matters into consideration, "my Lords" determined to ask Parliament to provide a sum of £500 for each volume of the debates of not less than 960 pages, or 60 sheets. This arrangement was carried out till 1885, and was then renewed for a further term of three years. Before the term had expired, notice was given by the Government of the day to terminate the arrangement, and tenders were invited for the reporting and printing of the parliamentary debates. Mr. Hansard was among those who tendered, but was not successful. The lowest tender was accepted,—that of a Limited Company (Macrae, Curtis and Co.), who engaged, without any subsidy whatever, to report the debates in both Houses, relying for their profit upon the sale of the parts and volumes to the Government and the public. The contractors were permitted to use their own discretion as to the fulness of the reports, provided that in no case should any speech be reported at less than one-third of its length, as delivered. Slips were to be delivered to the speakers for correction, to be returned in two days. The price fixed for a complete set of reports for one session was five guineas, and for a single part one shilling. Special reporters were to be in attendance, capable of reporting in full when necessary, but subject to this stipulation, the contractors could obtain their reports from such sources as they thought most convenient.

No special accommodation was provided for the reporters beyond that afforded in the reporters' galleries. But, after some time, the House of Lords resolved, on the motion of the Earl of Cadogan, "That Black-Rod be instructed to provide accommodation for the representative of Hansard's Debates [the old name was still retained by the new contractors,] within the precincts of the House of Lords." The motion was the result of a discussion respecting the report of a speech made by the Earl of Mar. It was generally admitted by the peers that the acoustic properties of the House were not good, and, that better accommodation was required, if the official shorthand writer was expected to supply a satisfactory report of the Debates. The Marquis of Salisbury, while complimenting the reporters on the way in which they generally exercised their functions, said he remembered several instances in which grave misapprehensions had arisen in consequence of the misreporting of Ministerial statements. In accordance with the resolution, a place was provided for Hansard's representative near the table occupied by the clerks of the House, and the seat has been retained with great advantage ever since. One of the conditions, however, of its occupation, is, that the shorthand writer is not to be relieved until he has been taking notes for four hours. As the transcript is not required to be completed until the following day, this restriction is not inconvenient, and as the sittings of the House of Lords are often very short, a single reporter can easily do the whole note-taking without any assistance.

It is singular that the House of Commons has not seen its way to afford similar accommodation to the official reporters, who are accordingly obliged to take their seats in the ordinary Reporters' Gallery, where it is impossible to hear, and therefore to report everything that takes place on the floor of the House. Set speeches, if distinctly uttered, may be fairly well heard and reported, but, when discussions arise on Clauses of Bills, or on matters of detail, which are commonly dealt with in a conversational style, it is rarely that the reporter can hear with sufficient certainty to present a faithful record.

The whole subject of official Parliamentary Reporting is in a state of transition. I have said that Hansard was superseded by Macrae, Curtis & Co., whose business was afterwards transferred to the now notorious Hansard Union, the collapse of which surprised no one who knew anything of printing and reporting. The result of the disaster which overtook the new Company, was, that further tenders were invited, and on this occasion the successful competitors were Reuter's Telegraph Company, who undertook both the reporting and the printing of the debates in consideration of a subsidy of £200 for each volume. The condition as to the length of the report was the same as before, except that every question addressed by a member to a Minister and the Minister's reply were to be given in full. The debates in Committee and on private bills were, as under the previous contract, to be reported as fully as debates on public questions, without regard to the hour of delivery of the speeches.

Many complaints were made as to the employment of a public Company of this character for such a purpose. Some of the oldest members of the Hansard staff declined to accept engagements under the new régime, and the result was, that fresh reporters were introduced. So much dissatisfaction, however, was expressed with the arrangement, and with the manner in which it had worked, that a Select Committee was appointed to take the matter into consideration and to report to the House; but the dissolution of 1892 followed almost immediately upon the appointment of the committee, and no report was presented. The subject is still in abeyance. Several previous committees have considered it and made recommendations. One of the main questions discussed has been whether the Official Report should be verbatim or abridged. The tendency has been to extend the reports, but Parliament has not insisted upon their being strictly verbatim. Questions of remuneration have also been considered by the committees, and discussions have taken place as to the desirability of the Government itself employing a special corps of official reporters. I confess I think that this would be the most satisfactory method of procedure. It works well in France and other countries, and has great advantages over the system of farming out the work to a particular individual or firm of contractors. In the French Chambers there is a very perfect method adopted. A double note is taken of all the debates by two sets of men, the ordinary reporters who take notes in turns of only two minutes, and the "revisers" who take notes for a quarter of an hour each, the duty of the latter being to revise the transcripts of the former. In this way great accuracy is secured, and the transcript is completed within a few minutes of the rising of the Chambers. This is an expensive but a very efficient mode. I cannot say that I think it necessary that all the speeches in our own Parliament should be reported in this duplicate manner, but I think it would be a decided advantage if a check-note were taken throughout (two or three good hands would suffice for the purpose) to which reference could be made when the regular reporter was in doubt as to a particular word or phrase, or as to the "fitting" of his turn. Two minutes' turns, are, I think, unnecessarily short, except perhaps toward the close of the proceedings. Five or ten minutes' turns would be better, requiring fewer changes, and enabling the reporter to get a better grasp of the subject. But, whatever arrangement may be made, it is absolutely essential that accommodation should be provided on the floor of the House, and I have little doubt that this will ultimately be conceded, as it has been in the Upper Chamber.

CHAPTER XIX.

THE PROFESSIONAL SHORTHAND WRITER.

THERE can be no question that the art of verbatim note-taking finds its highest development among the class of men to whom this chapter is devoted—professional Shorthand writers. In one sense of the word, everyone who writes Shorthand may be called a Shorthand writer. The term is a generic one, including the newspaper reporter, the Shorthand clerk or amanuensis, the legal Shorthand writer, and even the amateur who never earns a penny by the practice of his art. But in the specific and technical sense of the word, it is limited to the practitioner whose chief, if not exclusive, occupation is that of taking verbatim notes in the Law Courts or elsewhere, not necessarily for publication, but often for the private use of the clients by whom he is employed. Formerly, the distinction was more clearly marked than it is at the present time. For one Shorthand writer in the limited sense I have described, there are, perhaps, a hundred stenographers engaged in legal and commercial offices as salaried clerks, who have received the same designation. Some confusion arises from this similarity of title, and it is unfortunate that a more distinctive nomenclature has not been adopted. "Shorthand writer" and "reporter" were at one time thought sufficient to distinguish the two branches of the profession; but the advent of a third class, much more numerous than the other two combined, has introduced an element of confusion or uncertainty which should, if possible, have been avoided. The Shorthand writer pure and simple, the professional man who has his own clientèle, his own office and staff of assistants, considers himself as belonging to a class apart, and, without looking down upon either, objects to be classified with the newspaper reporter or the Shorthand clerk. The general public has but a hazy notion of these distinctions; but among the Shorthand fraternity they are well understood. The dividing line, however, between the reporter and the professional Shorthand writer is not so easily drawn as some may imagine. It is true that the reporter is usually attached to a newspaper establishment and receives a stipulated salary, while the Shorthand writer occupies a less dependent position, and, like the lawyer or the doctor, lives upon his professional fees. But there are reporters who are "unattached," who work entirely on their own account, and not a few of these undertake Shorthand engagements, legal or otherwise, which more commonly fall into the hands of the Shorthand writer proper. And even "attached" reporters sometimes obtain employment of this character to fill up their leisure hours. On the other hand, many Shorthand writers, whose time is not wholly occupied in their special department, accept reporting engagements for the Press, for which they are paid, not by salary, but according to an agreed tariff. Thus, though the nature of the work and its mode of remuneration may be easily distinguished, the same cannot always be said of the workers. They often overlap; their functions blend, and no sharp line of demarcation is possible between them. I know that there are members of each class who stand upon their dignity, and resent any intrusion into their own domain. Caste is not confined to the Hindoo. The Shorthand writer who prides himself upon his scrupulous verbal accuracy, is apt to look with disdain upon the man who is not so fettered, and who may have to condense into a column what ought to fill a newspaper page; while the reporter, rejoicing in a latitude unknown to his brother, pities the bondage of the latter, and tells you, with a soupçon of superciliousness, "He is only a Shorthand writer, don't you know?"

The attitude on both sides is utterly indefensible. I have done my best to combat it, but not always with success. If the Shorthand writer, by his greater practice, has acquired, as he probably has done, greater skill in his special field of labor, he ought to be ready to acknowledge the admirable manner in which the reporter, when the necessity arises, summarizes long speeches into a few paragraphs. And the reporter should be equally willing to recognize the special merits of his brother scribe, to whom the art of condensation is not as familiar as it is to himself.

It is, however, the greatest mistake to suppose that efficiency in one department necessarily means incapacity or deficiency in the other. Some newspaper reporters are excellent verbatim Shorthand writers, and can turn out as good a "transcript" of their notes as many of their more strictly professional colleagues. And I know many verbatim Shorthand writers who could, if required, produce as succinct and neat a summary of a speech or a case in Court, as the most experienced reporter on the *Times* or the *Daily News.* There is no necessary incompatibility, as is sometimes supposed, between the two departments of reporting work. I am not sure that the practitioner of each class would not find it an advantage to have a certain familiarity with the work of the other. The Shorthand writer who never does anything but verbatim note-taking, when finding himself hard pressed and under the necessity of omitting something, is not likely to omit so judiciously as he would do if he had been accustomed to take abbreviated reports and note down only the really important words or sentences that reach his ear. And the reporter who is nearly always condensing, will find it difficult to drop the habit when, on some special occasion, he is called upon to give a full report.

The information contained in this chapter is intended for both the classes to which I have referred; the newspaper reporter who desires to qualify himself for any outside shorthand work that may fall in his way, and the student who wishes to devote himself mainly or exclusively to professional shorthand writing. Many a work has been written with a view of assisting reporters in their earlier efforts; but I am not aware of any which has dealt in a comprehensive way with the duties of the Shorthand writer, and it will be my object in these pages to supply the deficiency.

The most important and probably the most extensive department under this head is legal shorthand writing. And as all the great law courts of the land are situated in London, Edinburgh and Dublin, it is at these centres that the professional shorthand writer finds his widest and most lucrative field of practice. The London shorthand writers are of course the most numerous, and they have formed themselves into a body, entitled, "The Institute of Shorthand Writers Practising in the Supreme Court of Judicature."

The objects of the Institute, as declared in the "Memorandum of Association," are: *(a)* The promotion of the more efficient practice of the art of Shorthand writing in connection with legal proceedings. *(b)* The raising of the qualifications and status of its members. *(c)* The doing all such other lawful things as are incidental or conducive to the attainment of the above objects. Provided always that it shall not be lawful for the Institute to impose on its members, or to support with its funds, any regulation which, if an object of the Institute, would make its registration under the Companies' Acts illegal." The first members of the Institute comprised all Shorthand writers practising in the Law Courts who desired to join, and who were admitted without examination. Any person now applying for membership must satisfy the Council that he has been as an articled pupil or assistant in the office of a member or members for not less than five years. He must also furnish evidence of having had a good general education, and having passed one of the following examinations:—Oxford or Cambridge, Senior or Junior Local; University of London Matriculation; College of Preceptors, first class or second class (first or second division) or "any other examination which the Council may deem of equivalent value as an educational test;" all certificates to include Latin and Mathematics. He is further required to pass an examination in practical note-taking in Court under the direction of the examiners. The Council, however, have power in special cases to admit, by a vote of not less than two-thirds of the whole Council, at a duly convened meeting, a candidate who may be unable to comply with the foregoing provisions. Any system of shorthand may be written by a candidate, his competency being tested by the accuracy with which he reads or transcribes his notes. The entrance fee is two guineas, and the annual subscription is one guinea. The Council consists of nine members.* The President, who is chosen annually, and is elected for one year only, must have been in practice as a shorthand writer on his own account for

---

* The present members of the Council (1892) are:—Messrs. A. R. Marten (President), W. C. Henderson, J. G. Hodges, T. A. Reed, H. H. Tolcher, H. M. Walsh, A. T. Wright, T. R. Wright. The Secretary is Mr. M. Levy, and the office is at 5 Mitre Court, Fleet Street, E.C.

at least ten years. Three members of the Council retire annually, but are eligible for re-election. The present office of the Institute is 5, Mitre Court, Fleet Street, E.C.

Nearly all the practising shorthand writers in the Courts are members of the Institute; and they hold occasional meetings at which matters of professional interest are discussed. The Institute has been officially recognised in various ways, and in certain cases no one but a member is permitted to take notes.

It will be seen from the preceding paragraph that the system of apprenticeships or articled-pupilships, if the term is admissable, prevails among professional shorthand-writers. The period of service contemplated by the rules of the Institute is five years; but it is sometimes shortened to three or four, according to the age of the pupil and his acquirements. If he begins young, say at 16, and has no knowledge of shorthand, the longer period is usually required; but if he is more advanced in years, and has made some progress with his shorthand, a year or two less may suffice. This is always a matter of arrangement. So also is the premium paid, which may vary from say £50 to £100. As a rule no salary is paid for the first year or two, but towards the end of the term, according to its length, a small salary may be given, or an allowance may be made for work done in over-time, say after six o'clock in the evening. No one should enter the profession by this or any other channel who has not a fairly good constitution, and cannot endure an occasional strain of hard work and long hours. At busy periods the work of note-taking and transcribing is very onerous, and may sometimes extend to midnight or even later. In former days it was a common experience with shorthand writers as well as reporters to spend the entire night in transcribing notes taken during the day. Now that the assistance of "dictatees" is more easily obtained—thanks to the more general study of Phonography among young men—these excessively long hours are rare; but when all the Law Courts are sitting, when Parliamentary Committees are in full swing, together with many other functions, at which the stenographer's presence is needed, it is not at all unusual for him to be engaged for days and weeks together from nine or ten in the morning till eleven or twelve at night in the laborious work of note-taking, dictating, or transcribing, or all three in turn. It is true that in slack periods there are ample opportunities for rest and recreation. The "Vac.," as the Long Vacation is termed, is a prolonged one, and a holiday of several weeks may be safely relied on, as well as a shorter period at Easter and Christmas. But notwithstanding these advantages, the strain of continuous labour such as I have described, is a severe one, and should only be undertaken by those who are physically as well as mentally qualified. I do not say that a robust frame is needed, but certainly the occupation is not suitable to a delicate constitution. With temperate and careful habits, attention to diet, and sufficient exercise, there is nothing in the work from which a person with an ordinary physique need shrink.

With these preliminaries understood, let me now introduce the young articled pupil to the duties on which he is about to enter. The office of his principals is probably somewhere in the neighbourhood of the Law Courts, and during the working season he has to be at his desk at half-past nine or ten in the morning. If he knows nothing of shorthand, his first duty will be to acquire the elements of the art, which will be taught him by his principal, or one of his assistants or advanced pupils. It will be some weeks or months before he can turn his knowledge to practical account. As soon as he can read the reporting style, he may be required to transcribe the shorthand notes of his seniors, if this mode of procedure is followed in the office. To do this with efficiency, he will have to exercise something more than the mere mechanical art of transcription. In the case of evidence given in the form of question and answer, there is little to be done beyond transcribing the words as they appear in the note-book; but with speeches and discussions, a good deal of discretion is needed. Ill-constructed sentences must be put, I do not say into elegant, but into grammatical English; they must, to use the technical expression, be "made to read." The extent to which verbal alterations are permitted or required will vary in different offices. Some shorthand writers are more fastidious in regard to the style of their transcripts than others. One man, with literary instincts, will take considerable liberties in this respect; another, with a more scrupulous regard to verbal fidelity, will be comparatively indifferent to the construction of sentences and phrases, leaving many an awkward gap unfilled, and making no effort to disentangle the intricacies and complications which are so common even among speakers of repute. No rigid rule can be laid down on this subject. As I have said, evidence given on oath should be followed as closely as possible, without any attempt at correction or embellishment. But speeches should not be treated in the same way. Careful speakers may be reported almost verbatim; but to transcribe in the same way the words of a slovenly speaker, who scarcely utters a sentence without an awkward break or a grammatical blunder is, to my mind, a thing that no professional Shorthand writer should for a moment tolerate. The pupil will naturally be guided by his superiors in this and in other matters. But I think few will be found to favor a slavishly literal reproduction of speeches. Even judgments delivered from the Bench should not be exempt from the verbal revision to which I am referring. Not every judge is a Westbury, whose words and sentences naturally fall into harmonious grouping, and have therefore only to be taken down as uttered and faithfully transcribed. It is, of course, a matter of considerable delicacy to tamper with the solemn pronouncements of judicial authorities, even in so slight a way as I have indicated. But I am sure there is no Shorthand writer of long experience who has not often found himself absolutely compelled to take liberties with the phraseology even of eminent judges when pronouncing their decisions. The greatest care is needed not to alter the sentiments expressed; but to allow the sentences to pass in their original form, would, in many cases, be to expose the Shorthand writer to the imputation of inaccuracy and carelessness; since no one would dream of fastening on a high legal dignitary the clumsy and involved sentences attributed to him in the transcript. They often pass unnoticed when delivered *ab oro*, and it is only when they are crystallized into permanent shape in the reporter's note book, that their real character is revealed.

I have dwelt at some length on this subject, because I am anxious that the young practitioner, at the commencement of his career, should understand that although the reporting work on which he is engaged is generally understood to be of a verbatim character, a certain discretion not only may, but must be exercised in making the shorthand transcripts. And it is largely in the exercise of this discretion that the difference between an efficient and an inefficient Shorthand writer is revealed. The object to be sought is, to make as little alteration as possible in the words uttered, and at the same time to see that the sentences are complete and read with reasonable smoothness, but without any attempt at embellishment. The newspaper reporter, engaged as he so often is in the work of condensation, naturally does not consider himself so rigorously bound by the precise phraseology of the speaker as the professional Shorthand writer, whose record is supposed to be an exact one, and has often to be verified on oath.

The first year or more of the articled pupil's period of service will probably be occupied in transcribing the notes of others, or (if this is not the custom of the office) taking notes himself from dictation and making the necessary transcripts. These should be written in a clear, bold hand: I do not mean the round, characterless hand of the law-writer, but a hand which, while preserving the characteristics of an educated person, shall be perfectly distinct and legible. A slovenly, even though accurate, transcript is always a discredit to the office from which it emanates. The transcript should also be properly punctuated; and, in the case of speeches, divided into paragraphs. It is usually made on foolscap paper specially prepared for Shorthand writers, margins being ruled off at both sides and also at the top and bottom of each page. Both sides of the paper are used, and when the transcript is completed it is placed in a stiff paper cover, also supplied by the law-stationers, and fastened with the orthodox red tape or the more modern paper-fastener.

CHAPTER XX.

IN THE LAW COURTS.

THE period at which the pupil is entrusted with the duty of taking notes in Court will mainly depend upon himself. As soon as he is qualified for the task, his principal will only be too glad to avail himself of his services. He should, of course, seek every opportunity of practising in court or elsewhere. Writing from dictation, though good practice in its way, is not the same thing as taking down the words of a speaker. Many a young shorthand scribe who has been most industrious in his "speed practice," and has gained a good certificate from his examiners, has found himself in an awkward predicament when he has, perhaps for the first time, exercised his pen by endeavouring to take down a moderately rapid speech in a law court, or, worse still, a discussion between counsel and the bench on some abstruse point of law. This requires not only manual dexterity, but considerable concentration of effort, and some familiarity with legal subjects and modes of procedure, which can only be acquired by special practice. The two-hundred-words-a-minute certificate and all that it implies, will be of little avail without the practical experience to which I have alluded. No opportunity, therefore, should be neglected of taking notes in Court or elsewhere. If the pupil is waiting in Court, with nothing to do, it is far better that he should be practising his note-taking than sitting idly with his note-book before him, making no effort to attain the skill without which he will assuredly make no mark in his profession. Many precious hours are thus wasted in the early period of service which might be utilized to the greatest advantage. Before being allowed to take notes by himself, except for practice, the beginner is usually required to write in conjunction with another, with the assistance of whose notes he is expected to make an accurate transcript. If he has been diligent and attentive, he will gradually be able to dispense with the aid of a senior hand. He may, for example, be permitted to "take" alone the evidence of an easy witness or the speech of a slow speaker; and, if he is successful in this, he will by degrees be entrusted with more difficult work. Everything, as I have said, will depend upon himself. His efficiency will soon be discovered, and ample opportunities will be afforded him of displaying it. Thoroughly good note-takers who can be relied on to make accurate and intelligible transcripts are not too numerous, and if a field is open to them their reputation is soon established, and employment is not difficult to secure.

The field of a legal or professional Shorthand writer's labours is a wide one. Though carried on mainly in a single building, they extend to a considerable number of Courts, necessitating the employment of numerous hands. There are two Courts of Appeal generally sitting, one or more Divisional Courts, the Divorce and Admiralty Courts, and the ordinary Courts of the Chancery and Queen's Bench Divisions. The Appeal Courts are usually presided over by three Judges, the Divisional Courts by two, and each of the other Courts by a single Judge. The Appeal Courts are the most difficult for the Shorthand writer. Intricate points of law are constantly brought before them, and the discussions upon them between the Bench and the bar are sometimes extremely difficult to follow. To the inherent difficulty of the subject under discussion there is often added the difficulty of hearing what is said, especially by judges who lean back in their chairs and take little pains to articulate their words with distinctness. The most experienced Shorthand writers are at times puzzled with these rapid conversations—for so they may be called—carried on by some half-a-dozen persons, two or three sometimes speaking at once; and an unskilled or inexperienced hand would be utterly appalled by the task of giving anything like a verbatim report of the proceedings which should be satisfactory to his client. The Divisional Courts are not much better. But a great deal depends upon the particular Judges who preside in them. Some are extremely popular among Shorthand reporters, alike constructing their sentences with perfect accuracy and pronouncing their words with great clearness and reasonable deliberation; while others, hardly uttering a complete sentence, and taking no trouble to speak distinctly, are the terror of the stenographic fraternity, who are expected to evolve order out of chaos, and present a perfectly intelligible transcript of what has only been half heard and still less understood. Long practice and familiarity with the work alone suffice to enable the Shorthand writer to meet with tolerable success the exigencies of the case.

In very difficult cases of this sort it is not uncommon for two Shorthand writers to take notes together. Sitting in different parts of the Court, one may hear what the other has missed, and by comparing notes deficiencies may be supplied which might be inevitable with a single note. This is especially the case with important judgments, in which, of course, the greatest accuracy is needed. Where a Shorthand writer is engaged on each side, there is necessarily a duplicate note taken (unless one deputes his colleague to act for him), and in such cases they should, wherever practicable, sit apart for the reason I have stated. In the ordinary Queen's Bench and Chancery Courts with a single Judge presiding, the task of note-taking is usually not so troublesome, there being less likelihood of several persons speaking at once or overlapping each other. But there is the same difference between judges and counsel as in the other Courts, some being perfectly easy and others extremely difficult to follow. The recording of evidence, unless it be of a very technical character, is generally regarded as the easiest kind of note-taking for the Shorthand writer. The questions and answers may rapidly follow each other, but they are almost always fairly intelligible, and involve no great difficulty in construction. The Judge, moreover, often takes a note of the evidence himself, and this tends to check the speed and give the Shorthand writer more breathing time than he can get when following a set speech. But great care is needed in taking and transcribing the evidence of witnesses—far more so than in reporting the speeches of counsel. Evidence is given on oath, and the Shorthand writer's transcript of it is often referred to, not only during the trial, when any doubt arises as to what has been said, or when Counsel wishes to quote it in support of an argument, but at subsequent stages, as when the case comes to be dealt with by a superior Court. If in such cases the transcript is found to be faulty, discredit is thrown upon the Shorthand writer, and, indeed, upon shorthand notes generally, and unpleasant remarks are made by both Judges and Counsel.

When a Judge writes his judgment and reads it in Court, his MS. can often be borrowed by the Shorthand writer and copied. But it is not safe to rely upon it. Even when it is certain that the Judge's notes can be obtained, the Shorthand writer should take it down fully. The Judge may not strictly follow his notes. He may make some additions to them in his oral judgment, and if these are not recorded the report will be an imperfect one. Or the Judge may write an illegible hand, and there may be great difficulty in deciphering it without the aid of the shorthand note. I have often known this to be the case with the MS. notes of a public speaker, and if entire reliance had been placed upon them they would have been almost useless.

The recognition of shorthand notes by the Judges can hardly be said to stand on a satisfactory footing. I can well remember the time when many Judges would absolutely refuse to listen to them, and decline to hear any note of evidence or argument that was not made either by Judge or by Counsel. Happily, that is a state of things that no longer exists. The value of an accurate shorthand note of evidence, and of summings-up and judgments delivered from the Bench has become so manifest that it is now generally recognized. Some Judges, before a case begins, will inquire if a Shorthand writer has been engaged, and if the answer is in the affirmative will content themselves with taking a very brief note of the evidence for their own use instead of the full note which they find necessary in the absence of a stenographic record. The public time thus saved is a strong additional argument in favor of shorthand notes. But there are still Judges of a more conservative type who rather discourage the employment of Shorthand writers. Yet even these, when a serious question arises as to the exact words that have been used by a witness or by a Judge, are often glad to be able to refer to the Shorthand writer's transcript, and will even go so far as to ask for its production, though, at a later stage, they may disallow the costs incurred in connection with it. In the Court of Appeal it is now customary to allow the costs of the shorthand notes of the judgment appealed against in the Court below, but not of the evidence, unless some special reason can be shown for it. The practice on this subject can hardly be said to be settled, different judges taking different views as to the extent to which the costs of notes should be allowed between the parties.* Some judges who have, from experience, formed a high opinion as to the value of shorthand notes in the administration of justice, have strongly advocated the appointment of official Shorthand writers to all the Superior Courts whose duty it should be to take notes of all the proceedings, not necessarily for transcription in every case, but to secure a permanent record for reference whenever the occasion should arise. In a few Courts such appointments have already been made—viz., in the Probate and Divorce Court, the Admiralty Court, and the Bankruptcy Court, where a Shorthand writer is constantly in attendance to take notes of the trials for the use of the Judges and the parties concerned. There are many arguments in favor of such an arrangement, but it does not find favour with Shorthand writers generally, who prefer the greater independence connected with their present position to any official status that they might acquire by a Court appointment. They think that by a suitable arrangement as to the allowance of the cost of notes on taxation, all the advantages of official appointments might be secured without any alteration of the existing system, under which Shorthand writers receive their instructions from the solicitors engaged in the litigation.

When the articled pupil's period of service is ended, it is of course open to him to commence business on his own account, or to accept a position as assistant in the office in which he has been articled or any other where an engagement may be offered him; and he may, according to arrangement, receive a fixed stipend or be paid *pro rata* for the work that he does. The latter is, perhaps, the commonest method adopted in Shorthand writers' offices, a certain minimum amount per annum being guaranteed by the principals. Beginners do not often enter into business entirely on their own account, unless they have some connection or interest which will ensure them a moderate income. They commonly find it more advantageous, at first at any rate, to enter a well-established office as assistants; or, if they prefer a more independent position, they lay themselves

* See "Shorthand Notes and the Practice relating to them: being a Collection of Cases decided in Courts of Justice." By Matthias Levy. 1886.

out to undertake work for other Shorthand writers, who, in busy seasons, are often glad to secure the services of well-qualified outsiders. The chief business naturally comes from solicitors, not from their clients, and for this reason young Shorthand writers seeking employment endeavour to cultivate the acquaintance of the legal fraternity. Most large legal offices employ a particular firm of Shorthand writers in all cases requiring notes to be taken; and in such cases it is rightly considered a breach of professional etiquette for others to offer their services and endeavour to supplant their more fortunate brethren of the pen. In other and smaller offices, where the engagement of a Shorthand writer is a comparatively rare occurrence, there may be no regular employment of one firm or individual, in which case there can be no impropriety in making application when a favourable opportunity arises. Nor is there any good reason why a Shorthand writer should not seek instructions from clients themselves whom they happen to know, when they are engaged in litigation. It is, after all, the client who pays the bill, and he has as much right to express a desire to have a particular Shorthand writer engaged as to wish to retain the services of a particular counsel. There is among Shorthand writers the same keen competition as is found in other professions, and it sometimes leads to the same kind of friction and unpleasantness. But, as a rule, it is honourably conducted, and in such a manner as not to interfere with friendly intercourse and professional co-operation whenever it is desirable and practicable. And this is an important consideration which should never be overlooked. Two Shorthand writers, it may be, are engaged in the same case: one, say, for the plaintiff and one for the defendant. If both are instructed to transcribe their notes, their labor may be greatly facilitated by co-operation. They can refer to each other's notes in doubtful cases, where one, for example, has failed to catch with certainty a word or sentence that the other may have heard better, and therefore recorded more accurately; or, in specially difficult cases, they may dictate their notes conjointly, and arrange for duplicate copies, lessening both labor and expense, and at the same time securing uniformity in the transcripts, thus preventing the unpleasant observations occasionally heard in Court when some slight discrepancy has been discovered in the notes of the Shorthand writers engaged. Such discrepancies are inevitable under the conditions in which legal discussions are often conducted and shorthand notes taken; but no allowance is made for the special difficulties that have to be encountered. Hence the desirability of friendly co-operation wherever it can be secured. It cannot, of course, be expected that a competent Shorthand writer will consent to co-operate with one who is manifestly and admittedly incompetent; but assuming that both are fairly qualified, every effort should be made to work in collaboration without any nice adjustment of claims to superiority.

Before leaving the subject of Court reporting, I may mention one or two points of practical interest in connection with it. The authorities cited in the course of legal arguments at the bar and on the bench are very numerous, and the references are sometimes difficult to obtain. The regular "Law Reports," now published officially and constantly quoted, can be easily procured; but the earlier reports (some in black letter) are scarce and not readily accessible. The Shorthand writer should be familiar with their names, and be careful, in note-taking, to take the references accurately. The ordinary reports can be referred to in the Courts themselves while they are sitting, or they can at times be borrowed from the counsel or solicitors engaged in the case. There is also a library of these and other books of reference belonging to the Institute of Shorthand Writers, to which the members of that body have access—a valuable privilege, of which they very frequently avail themselves. In regard to quotations generally, let me add a word of advice. It is not enough to take only the first few words of a quotation and the last, without any indication of the intermediate part. The Shorthand writer who adopts this method may find that his first and last words are several pages apart, although he may be certain that only a few sentences have been read. The natural inference is that the speaker must have skipped a great deal; and nothing is more common than such fragmentary quotation. The only safe plan, if it is found difficult or tiresome to take a verbatim note of a long quotation, is to write frequent catch-words, so as to be enabled to trace the parts read when the book is obtained, and thus to avoid the transcription of entire sentences which have never been uttered. It is not always easy to distinguish between the speaker's words and the quoted passage. Remarks are interjected as to which it is doubtful whether they come from the speaker or the writer; and unless a pretty continuous, not necessarily verbatim, note is taken of these citations, the reporter may be at a loss as to the use of his inverted commas, and attribute the words uttered to the wrong persons. This remark, though specially applicable to legal note-taking, may also be applied to many other kinds of reporting in which quotations abound. It is always desirable to obtain the speaker's citations, if he has them, or at any rate to get the references and verify them whenever it is possible, unless the reporter is perfectly certain that he has taken them down correctly. Nothing is commoner than for a speaker to misread a word in such cases or to skip a line or two, and without a reference to the original, accuracy cannot be secured

CHAPTER XXI.

OTHER SPHERES OF LABOR.

I HAVE said that most of the work of the professional Shorthand writer is carried on in the Law Courts. But this is not by any means the only sphere of his labours. Arbitrations and references offer a wide field for the exercise of his special functions; and as they are often very prolonged, they are among the most lucrative branches of his business. It is true that they usually spring out of proceedings initiated in court, but they are generally held elsewhere—sometimes in London and sometimes in the country. The proceedings at an arbitration are very similar to those of a court of law. The arbitrator is the Judge, and he is usually attended by counsel on both sides. Occasionally there are two arbitrators and an umpire. Speeches are made and witnesses examined as in Court; the decision, however, is given not orally, as by a Judge, but in the form of a written award. The parties are generally seated round a large table, and the Shorthand writer has rarely any difficulty in securing a good seat near the arbitrator where he can hear all that is said. This can hardly be said in the case of the Law Courts, where the seats of the Shorthand writers and reporters are at an inconvenient distance from the Bench, so that when a judgment is delivered by a Judge whose elocution is not very distinct, the Shorthand writer who has to "take" is compelled to stand and write at the Registrar's table.

Shorthand notes are also taken of evidence given before Masters, Referees, and other Court officials. This may be regarded as a branch of Court reporting; and in some instances it is of so important a character that the Shorthand writer is sworn before taking notes. He is thus, in a sense, a servant of the Court, and is bound to do his work faithfully. His note is in such cases accepted as the authorized record of the proceedings. He is always provided with a good seat, and if he has not distinctly heard an answer he may ask the witness to repeat it. Evidence taken "on commission" is also occasionally taken down by means of Shorthand, but it is more commonly recorded by the Commissioner himself.

During the sitting of Parliament a large number of Committees of both Houses hold their sittings, and require the attendance of Shorthand writers to record the evidence given by the witnesses, which is always printed from day to day, copies being laid on the table at the beginning of each sitting. This work has for several generations been entrusted to the Messrs. Gurney, who employ a large and competent staff for the purpose; but, when a pressure of work arises, they occasionally resort to other efficient and well-known Shorthand writers for the assistance they require. No notes are recognized by the Committee but those of the official Shorthand writer; but occasionally, in the case of "Select Committees," the evidence before whom is only published in the form of a Blue-Book at the end of the inquiry, an independent Shorthand writer is engaged to take notes of the evidence for persons who are unwilling to wait for the appearance of the official record. He has always, however, the disadvantage of an inferior seat to that occupied by the recognized reporter, who, as I have already mentioned in an earlier chapter, is seated at a little table in front of the chairman, at which also sits the witness, who can be checked when necessary and asked to repeat an answer imperfectly heard or understood. In addition to the evidence, the speeches of counsel are sometimes reported, not so much for the use of the Committee as of the parties promoting the particular bills under consideration. None but a highly-skilled Shorthand writer should undertake work of this character. The printed transcript is closely scrutinized, and used by Counsel in their speeches and arguments before the Committee; and even in the course of the proceedings reference is often made to the Shorthand writer's notes, which he is called upon to read to settle some point in dispute as to the statement of a witness. When the evidence and speeches on a particular bill are ended, the committee-room is cleared; but the official Shorthand writer remains with the Committee, that he may, if necessary, read any portion of his notes to which they may desire to refer. When the decision on the preamble is given, the clauses of the bill are gone through. This is often a matter of form; but when opposition is offered there is occasionally a severe struggle over particular clauses, and evidence is taken upon them, which has to be recorded in the same way as the evidence upon the preamble. The proceedings in Committees of the House of Lords are much the same as in the Commons. The witnesses, however, do not sit at a central table, but stand at a side desk, under which the Shorthand writer sits to take notes. In Messrs. Gurney's office the custom is for the Shorthand writer's notes to be taken away at intervals, and dictated or transcribed by assistants trained for the purpose, the transcript being, of course carefully revised by the Shorthand writer himself before being sent to the printers. The same practice is adopted in some other offices; but in many cases the Shorthand writer prefers to dictate his notes himself. This, of course, can only be done when the day's proceedings are ended, unless (as is frequently the case) he is relieved by a colleague and leaves at an earlier period.

The old Election Committees, formerly appointed to try election petitions, are now a thing of the past. They were often very protracted, and the evidence taken before them was very voluminous. So important were the proceedings deemed that the Shorthand writer was always sworn before being permitted to take notes. The function of these Committees is now discharged by another tribunal. Two of Her Majesty's Judges hear all election petitions, and report to the Speaker of the House of Commons the decision at which they arrive, to which is appended a transcript of the evidence taken by the official Shorthand writers who accompany them, and who, as in the case of the Election Committees, are sworn to take a faithful note of the proceedings. These trials were at one time very numerous, and required a great many Shorthand writers to record them; but, owing largely to the extremely stringent measures against bribery and corruption at elections, these offences are now comparatively rare, and consequently very few petitions are presented.

The Assizes, held periodically in different parts of the country, form another fruitful field of labor for the Shorthand writer. One or more of the fraternity attend each circuit. In olden days they commonly went the entire round of the circuit with the Judges, returning to London when it was ended. Now that even distant country towns can be reached in a few hours, it is no difficult matter to go backwards and forwards as the necessity may arise. It is not often that criminal trials at Assizes are taken by the professional Shorthand writer, but his services are frequently called into requisition at civil trials, which resemble in all respects those held in London. It rarely happens, however, that the transcript of the notes is required from day to day. Indeed, in many cases, this would be a matter of great difficulty, if not impossibility. Where only one shorthand-writer (I am not now referring to newspaper reporters) is present and engaged all day in taking notes of a case—say, up to five or six o'clock), it is obvious that he cannot have his transcript ready by the following morning. In large cities like Liverpool and Manchester, where efficient assistance can be obtained, there is but little difficulty in the supply of a daily transcript. If it is required in smaller towns, it is usual to take down a small corps of note-takers and dictatees for the purpose. Occasionally the newspaper reporters receive commissions to take notes of assize cases; but more frequently London Shorthand writers are employed, as being more familiar with the work, and being better known to the solicitors, who are in the habit of engaging their services. They are also better able to produce their notes in London when they are required. Assize cases are frequently adjourned to London for the determination of legal points that have arisen, either by way of "further consideration" by the Judge who has tried them, or by way of appeal to the superior Courts; and in such cases it is found convenient to employ the same Shorthand writer throughout. Many cases, too, that are tried at the Assizes arise out of litigation which has been initiated in London and in which a London Shorthand writer has been engaged. It is natural, therefore, that he should be retained for the country trial, especially if it is on the circuit which he is in the habit of attending.

Before leaving the subject of legal reporting, it may be convenient that, for the information and guidance of the inexperienced, I should indicate the manner in which the headings of legal and other transcripts are worded and set out. There are slight differences in the forms adopted in different Shorthand writers' offices; but these are unimportant, and the subjoined forms may be taken as a sufficient guide:—

HOUSE OF LORDS.

July 22nd, 1892.

COWLEY (Pauper) ....Appellant
and
NEWMARKET LOCAL BOARD ....Respondents.

Present—

The Lord Chancellor
Lord Herschell
Lord Hannen.

[Transcript of the shorthand notes of Messrs. A. and B., 90, Chancery Lane, W.C.]

Counsel for the Appellant: Mr. Joseph Brown, Q.C., and Mr. Williams.

Counsel for the Respondents: The Solicitor-General and Mr. Fellowes.

[At the end.]

Questions put.

That the order appealed from be reversed.

The non-contents have it.

That this appeal be dismissed.

The contents have it.

COURT OF APPEAL.

Supreme Court of Judicature.
In the Court of Appeal
Queen's Bench Division.

Royal Courts of Justice;
Feb. 4, 1892.

Before
The Master of the Rolls,
Lord Justice Bowen, and
Lord Justice Kay.

EASTON AND CO.

v.

NAR VALLEY DRAINAGE COMMISSIONERS.

[Transcript, &c.]
Counsel for the Appellants, &c.

DIVISIONAL COURT.

High Court of Justice.
Queen's Bench Division,
Divisional Court.

Royal Courts of Justice;
July, 17th, 1892.

Before

Mr. Justice Grantham and
Mr. Justice Collins.

STANDARD INSURANCE CO. *v.* HEPBURN.

[Transcript, &c.]

Counsel, &c.

HIGH COURT OF JUSTICE.

High Court of Justice,
Chancery Division.

Royal Courts of Justice;
June 3, 1892.

Before

Mr. Justice Romer.

FREEMANTLE *v.* APPLETON.

[Transcript, &c.]

Counsel for the Plaintiff, &c.

ASSIZES.

High Court of Justice,
Queen's Bench Division.

Norfolk Summer Assizes,
Norwich; July 20th, 1891.

Before

Mr. Justice Hawkins
and a
Special Jury.

GREEN *v.* MELLOR.

[Transcript, &c.]

Counsel for the Plaintiff: Mr. Jones, Q.C., and Mr. Smith.
Counsel for the Defendant: Mr. Rogers, Q.C., and Mr. Brown.

[At the end of a trial.]

The Jury consulted (or the Jury retired to consult).
On their return into Court,
The Associate: Gentlemen, are you agreed upon your verdict?
The Foreman: Yes.
The Associate: Do you find for the Plaintiff or the Defendant?
The Foreman: For the Plaintiff.
The Associate; What damages?

The Foreman; Three hundred and twenty pounds.
Mr. Jelf: I ask your Lordship for judgment.
Mr. Justice Vaughan Williams: Yes.
Mr. Jelf: Will your Lordship certify for a special jury?
Mr- Justice Vaughan Williams: Yes.

BANKRUPTCY COURT.

In the High Court of Justice.
In Bankruptcy.
At Bankruptcy Buildings, Carey Street, W.C.
The day of 1892.

Before Mr. Registrar

Re No. of 189

Ex-parte The Official Receiver.

Public Examination of the Debtor.

Transcript from the Shorthand Notes of Mr. of Official Shorthand Writer to the Court of Bankruptcy.

Mr. appeared as the Official Receiver.

Mr. Q.C., and Mr. of Counsel, instructed by Messrs. Solicitors, of appeared on behalf of the Trustee.

Mr. of Counsel, instructed by Mr. Solicitor, of appeared on behalf of the Debtor.

Mr. appeared as Solicitor for Mr. a Creditor.

Mr. a Creditor, appeared in person.

A—— B—— the above-named debtor being sworn and examined at the time and place above mentioned, upon his oath saith in answer to the questions proposed to him as follows :—

Examined by Mr.

Q.
A. &c.

The usual question having been asked as to whether any creditor desired to put any further questions to the debtor, and there being no response, the learned Registrar declared the examination to be concluded.

The Debtor was directed to attend at the Court on the day of for the purpose of reading and signing this examination.

The following declaration is made by the Official Shorthand Writer :—

"I, A. B., of................. one of the Official Shorthand Writers appointed to this Court, do solemnly and sincerely declare that I will truly and faithfully take down the questions and answers put to and given by persons to be examined in this matter, and will deliver true and faithful transcripts thereof as the Court may direct."

CENTRAL CRIMINAL COURT.

Central Criminal Court;
October 1, 1892.

Before Sir Charles Hall, Recorder.

REGINA
v.
THOMPSON, JONES, AND SMITH.

[Transcript, &c.]

Counsel for the Prosecution: The Attorney-General and Mr. Williams.
Counsel for Thompson; Mr. Jenkins.
Counsel for Jones: Mr. Walker.
Counsel for Smith: Mr. Perkins.

SESSIONS.

Middlesex Quarter Sessions.

Sessions House;
Before Monday, 25th March, 1892.
Sir Peter Edlin (Assistant Judge), and
P. B. Burgess, Esq., and
Loveland Loveland, Esq. (Magistrates).

THE MIDLAND RAILWAY COMPANY............Appellants
v.
THE ASSESSMENT COMMITTEE OF THE HENDON UNION AND THE OVERSEERS OF THE PARISH OF WILLESDEN..............Respondents.

[Transcript from the Shorthand Notes, &c.]

Mr. Littler, Q.C., Mr. Castle, and Mr. Ernest Page appeared as Counsel for the Appellants, instructed by Messrs.

Mr. Staveley Hill, Q.C., M.P., Mr. Poland, Q.C., and Mr. E. R. Bartley Denniss appeared as Counsel for the Respondents, instructed by

PATENT CASE.

Royal Courts of Justice;
Wednesday, July 31st, 1892.

Before the Comptroller-General of Patents, &c.

In the matter of the Patents, Designs, and Trade Marks Acts, 1883 to 1888,
and
In the matter of the Application of John Smith for Letters Patent, No. 18,933 91
and
In the matter of the Opposition of J. W. Brown thereto.

[Transcript, &c.]

Mr. Asfield, Q.C., appeared as Counsel for the Applicant.
Mr. Lloyd White appeared as agent for the Opponent.

ROYAL COMMISSION.

Minutes of Evidence taken before the
ROYAL COMMISSION ON METROPOLITAN WATER SUPPLY.
First Day.
At Trafalgar Buildings, Charing Cross, S.W.,
Monday, 16th May, 1892.
Present
The Right Hon. Lord Balfour of Burleigh, Chairman.

Sir G. B. Bruce, Kt., C.E.
Sir A. Geikie, Kt., D.Sc., LL.D., F.R.S.
Professor J. Dewar, M.A., LL.D., F.R.S.
G. H. Hill, esq., C.E.
J. Mansergh, esq., C.E.
W. Ogle, esq., M.D.

Francis Gaskell, esq., Secretary.

[Transcript, &c.]

Mr. James Searle called and examined.

Chairman: Are you the clerk of the New River Water Company?—Yes. &c., &c.

COMPANY MEETING.

Minutes of Proceedings*
at the Half-Yearly Meeting of the
GREAT WESTERN RAILWAY COMPANY,
Held at the Paddington Station, January 5th, 1890.
.... in the Chair.

The Secretary read the notice convening the meeting.

The Secretary read the minutes of the last meeting, which were confirmed.

The report and statement of accounts were taken as read.

---

* An alternative form is "Great Western Railway Company, Report of Proceedings at," &c.

Among other engagements of the professional shorthand-writer, I may mention attendance at the meetings of public companies. In London especially there are numerous large companies—banking, railway, insurance, and the like—that usually employ Shorthand writers to take *verbatim* notes of the speeches, sometimes for publication and distribution among the shareholders, and sometimes to be filed in the office for future reference. These reports are occasionally printed in class journals devoted to special interests, and they may be taken by some member of the journalistic staff. But a large proportion of class-work of this and other kinds is done not by reporters attached to particular journals, but by unattached Shorthand writers from the law courts or practising in other branches of the profession. I have already referred to this kind of reporting in the chapter devoted to newspaper work, and most of my suggestions as to the manner in which it should be done will equally apply to the Shorthand writer, except that this functionary, unlike his brother of the press, has nothing to do in the way of condensing, his sole duty being to furnish a complete record of everything that has been said.

The meetings of Scientific Associations, at which discussions of a more or less technical character are held, afford ample scope for the higher kinds of Shorthand practice. Many of these Societies publish volumes of Transactions, which contain not only the papers read at their meetings, but reports of the discussions following them. The latter are sometimes given only in a very abridged form, but in some instances they are reported in great detail, almost, if not quite, verbatim, necessitating therefore the services of a thoroughly competent Shorthand writer. At the meetings of some of the Medical Societies, for example, highly technical matters are discussed, the reporting of which needs, on the part of the reporter, a great deal more than ordinary stenographic skill. Without some familiarity with the expressions employed and the subjects treated, the attempt to report them could only lead to hopeless failure. Discussions, again, on engineering, electrical, and other kindred topics abound in technicalities, that would utterly frustrate any endeavour on the part of one unaccustomed to them to report the speeches in which they occur. The Shorthand writer, therefore, who lays himself out for work of this description, should seek to qualify himself for the task by suitable reading and practice. I do not, of course, suggest that he should become a student, in the ordinary sense, of each of the subjects with which he may have to deal in his professional capacity. This would be an unreasonable, if not an impossible requirement. There are, however, many text-books on these subjects which he might read with advantage, if only to gain a general insight into their nature and terminology. Any expert could assist him in his selection. Nor would the knowledge thus acquired be limited to the special object in view. These technicalities frequently crop up on other and unexpected occasions (in law cases, for example), and then the reporter whose reading and practice have made them familiar to him, has a marked advantage over others not similarly qualified. What I have said on this subject in an earlier chapter should be taken to heart by the professional Shorthand writer as well as by the Shorthand clerk.

Lectures on scientific and technical subjects afford much the same kind of practice. They are the terror of the uninitiated, but are comparatively easy to the reporter who is accustomed to them. Lecturers themselves occasionally engage the services of a Shorthand writer to take down their addresses, which they have themselves no time to commit to writing. In these cases the difficulty is not quite so great, since there can be no objection to blanks being left here and there for unfamiliar expressions or descriptions of diagrams for the lecturer himself to supply in his revision. It is still easier when the reporter is employed, as he sometimes is, to take down the lecture from dictation before or after its delivery, in which case he can ask for any explanation or repetition that he may need in the course of his task.

Conferences and Congresses of every description come within the scope of the Shorthand writer's engagements as well as in those of the newspaper reporter. Nor are these confined to his own locality, or even to his own country. I have myself attended many such gatherings in all parts of the kingdom, on the continent, and in still more distant lands. This, perhaps, is one of the pleasantest sides of the Shorthand writer's occupation. Meetings of this character are generally held in the summer or autumn months, when travelling is an agreeable interlude to more serious work. An engagement of this kind affords ample opportunities of enlarging one's experience, indulging in harmless pastime, adding to one's collection of curios, and the like. To the reporter or Shorthand writer who knows how to use a sketch-book or a camera, such opportunities are most acceptable; nor are they less so to the disciple of Old Isaac, whose rod and basket are often packed up with his note-book; or to the geologist or antiquarian or any other specialist, who can thus find a new field for his researches.

Congresses and Conferences may be reported by the professional Shorthand writer, either for their promoters, or for special publications devoted to the subjects discussed. These class journals often require such services. They have commonly no reporters on their regular staff who are competent to undertake difficult shorthand work. It is but rarely, perhaps only two or three times a year, that a particular journal needs assistance of this kind, and a salaried reporter, therefore, would be out of the question. Accordingly the independent or unattached Shorthand writer finds in class-publications some of his best and most regular clients. Not only are his own services called into requisition, but those of his colleagues or assistants. Where the sittings are long, or several are held concurrently, a small staff is needed, which the Shorthand writer supplies from his own office (if he has one), or from among his professional brethren.

Sermon reporting is another branch of the stenographic profession which brings grist to the mill, and occupies many spare hours. But it almost needs a specialist to undertake it with satisfaction to himself and others. I have known many excellent Shorthand writers who would not hesitate at taking a difficult law case, but who would shudder at the notion of taking a verbatim report for publication of a sermon by a preacher of rather more than ordinary fluency, or having any peculiarity of style. Yet there are few shorthand students, who do not, in their early days, practise this branch of the art. The opportunity so often presents itself that it would be strange if advantage were not taken of it. To many, indeed, it is almost the only available opportunity for "keeping the hand in;" and it is found very effectual in accomplishing that object. Without the practice which the weekly sermon affords (or some equivalent), the fingers will easily lose their suppleness, and the mind its instantaneous perception of the forms of the words to be recorded. The amateur, therefore, who has but little time for reporting practice, and yet wishes to keep up the speed which he has attained, may be recommended to avail himself of this regularly occurring occasion; and even the reporter, who rarely needs to take a verbatim note (and there are many such), should not neglect it. I know that many will smile at the suggestion of a professional reporter taking notes for practice; but I make the recommendation notwithstanding. The practitioner in full swing may find it unnecessary, and may please himself in the matter. I am only referring to reporters (especially young ones,) who seldom use their shorthand at all, and then only for making casual notes for paragraphs or very condensed reports of speeches.

Nothing can be much easier than to report the sermons of some preachers who are slow in delivery and simple in style. Many a sermon of this character is delivered at not more than 80 words a minute, and could be taken down with ease by the veriest shorthand tyro. On the other hand, few things are more difficult than the reporting of a rapidly-delivered pulpit discourse of an ornate character, abounding, it may be, in historical allusions and scholarly references, beyond the range of ordinary reading, interspersed with poetical quotations from unmentioned authors. Yet I have known the task attempted—with what result may be imagined—by Shorthand writers possessing but a very meagre acquaintance with books, with barely sufficient Biblical knowledge to pass a Sunday-school examination, and wholly ignorant of theological matters generally. Without some familiarity with these subjects, sermon reporting *for professional purposes* should not be attempted. Here again, I do not desire to convey the impression that the reporter should be a theological expert. I am only contending that he should be sufficiently well read to be able to follow readily with mind and hand, the various points of an argumentative or historical discourse such as is occasionally delivered to intelligent and educated congregations. The failure to catch a single proper name, for example—say that of a German theologian or of an ancient father, or a Latin or Greek phrase, or some unusual expression not likely to be recognised by an indifferently educated person, may involve the omission of an entire sentence or more, and perhaps occasion a "solution of continuity" in the address which may impair its force or weaken its style. The most experienced and accomplished hand may now and then be at a loss owing to a failure of this kind; but he will know better how to deal with it than a less instructed scribe. In like manner, in case of a mis-hearing, or a failure to hear at all many words of an indistinct speaker, he will be better able to fill the gap intelligibly and reasonably; or if this be impossible or risky, to omit with discretion, and preserve, as far as may be, the continuity of the discourse. A want of familiarity with Biblical names is almost fatal to the successful practice of sermon-reporting. I knew an excellent Shorthand writer, and a man fairly well read in secular literature, who in reporting a sermon was nearly "bowled over" by a reference to Jannes and Jambres, and stumbled frightfully at Adoni-Bezek. It is easy to say that he could refer to his Concordance. That may be so if he has caught the sounds accurately; but every shorthand practitioner knows that unfamiliar names are not easily caught, and that if several occur together their sounds are mis-heard or unheard, and there is not even enough material left for a successful search among Concordances and Dictionaries. It is only the fairly-instructed man who knows how effectively to consult these aids, and no one who relies too much upon them is likely to make headway in his profession.

One difficulty in the way of the sermon-reporter is, that, as a rule, he has to write upon his knee. In America, there is in most large places of worship a reporters' pew, with every accommodation for writing. We have not advanced so far in this country. Many a preacher would be scandalized at the bare thought of such an innovation. Some ministers, like the late Dr. Punshon, strongly object to the reporting and publication of their sermons, and would, if they had the power, relegate the Shorthand writer and his note-book to the most distant seat in the gallery. Others have no such objection, and some extemporaneous speakers even employ Shorthand writers to take down their sermons, which they themselves revise and publish. Mr. Spurgeon was a conspicuous example of this; and for many years, almost from the commencement of his ministry in London, his Sunday morning sermons were published officially, from week to week, a few days after their delivery. Dr. Cumming's sermons were also reported in shorthand for himself and afterwards published, not separately, but collected into volumes, which had a wide circulation. Similar arrangements have been made by other preachers who have the gift of speech, but not of writing. In such cases, the reporter has, of course, proper accommodation provided for him; but the non-official Shorthand writer is only one of the general public, and is left to his own devices to obtain the best seat he can. In some churches or chapels he finds it necessary to be early in attendance to secure a seat near the pulpit, often the only place in which a satisfactory note can be taken. Few preachers can be heard well enough for a reporter's purpose unless he is within a few yards of the pulpit. Here and there a Boanerges arises, whose tones will penetrate every corner of the largest building, and who may be reported a hundred yards away. But he is a rare exception; and, unless the reporter knows his man, it is always best for him to assume that he is not a very distinct speaker, and to arrange accordingly. Let me also suggest that it is as well for the reporter to have his writing materials in readiness in good time. It is not safe to rely upon an introductory prayer from the preacher, or even a text. He will sometimes begin suddenly without either the one or the other, and if the reporter has not everything in readiness he may miss the opening sentences. He should also provide a sufficient quantity of paper for the longest sermon, especially in the evening, when ministers occasionally prolong their discourses to an inordinate length. I have several times reported sermons over two hours in delivery, and on one occasion, my paper running short, had to go over the ground again and write between the lines—of course, in very small characters. It is well to provide for possible, though improbable, contingencies such as these. If the preacher is known to be nervous, it is only kindness on the part of the reporter to keep, if possible, out of his sight. To some men the appearance of a note-book and a pen flying over its pages is very disconcerting, while to others it may positively act as a stimulus.

The usual tariff for shorthand writing is a guinea a day, or portion of a day, for attendance and taking notes, and 8d. per folio of 72 words for the transcript. In a few cases—viz., in the House of Lords, the Judicial Committee of the Privy Council, and the Committees of the House of Commons—the attendance fee is two guineas, the transcript in these cases being charged at 9d. per folio. The same fee is paid for taking notes at the Assizes, where the Shorthand writer, unless he is specially retained, attends at his own expense. At public meetings it is also usual to make a charge of a guinea for attendance, in addition to the usual 8d. per folio for the transcript Lectures and sermons are generally paid for at a somewhat less rate, being the subject of special agreement, according to the length or number of the addresses; or a fixed sum may be agreed upon irrespective of length. In the case of newspaper reports supplied by independent Shorthand writers or reporters, no attendance-fee is charged, the rate of payment being per column. A guinea is the customary charge for a *Times* column, which contains about 30 folios, or rather more than 2,000 words. Dictatees are paid at the rate of 2d. per folio for taking down and transcribing.

With regard to the ordinary charge of a guinea a day for taking notes, it has often been suggested that this fee should be regulated according to the length of the sitting. It may seem strange that the same charge should be made for five minutes' work as for an entire day. And where the transaction terminates, as it sometimes does, with a long day's note-taking, the fee is absurdly low for such skilled labor. Where, however, a transcript is ordered, the charge made for it is a fairly liberal one, and is some compensation for the inadequate payment for taking the notes. When the solicitors for the plaintiff and the defendant, instead of employing separate Shorthand writers, join in the expense of shorthand notes with a view of lessening the cost, one only is engaged, and he supplies a transcript, if ordered, to each side, charging 8d. per folio for the original and 4d. per folio for the copy, and debiting half the aggregate amount—*i.e.*, 6d. per folio and half the attendance-fee—to each client. If, however, the order comes, as it sometimes does, from two or more clients *independently*, the full fees are charged to each.

When travelling expenses have to be incurred, they are, of

course, paid by the employer, except when Shorthand writers are attending their own circuits, which (as I have already said) they do at their own cost. First-class railway fares and a reasonable sum for hotel expenses are generally charged; but in the case of some of the smaller country papers second-class fares only are allowed in addition to hotel expenses.

CHAPTER XXII.

Longhand and Type-writing.

I HAVE said but little on the subject of longhand in connection with the Shorthand writer's labors. It is nevertheless an important matter, and deserves special consideration. The rapidity with which newspaper reports and shorthand transcripts of every kind have to be produced is not conducive to the cultivation of a neat and clear caligraphy. When the object is to get a column or a "folio" completed in the shortest possible time, the writing almost inevitably acquires a running, dashing, if not sprawling style, which is generally inelegant and often illegible. There are some specially-gifted caligraphists, who, whatever their speed, always write neatly and clearly, and are the delight of the composing-room; while others hardly write a line that does not occasion some hesitation to the reader or the compositor. With this, as with all other accomplishments, there are great differences in the original endowment. To some persons it is perfectly easy and natural to write legibly and elegantly, and to these I have nothing to say, except that they ought to be thankful for a gift which saves the time and preserves the equanimity of their fellow-creatures, if it does not contribute to their absolute enjoyment. But to those—and there are many such—to whom the gift is denied, let me say that a great deal may be done in the required direction by care and attention. A bad writer should seek to discover, if he does not already know them, special features which need correction. It may be that he fails to distinguish his u's and n's, that i's, n's, u's, and m's are, as they stand, nothing but a series of unmeaning strokes, whose signification can only be guessed by the aid of the adjoining letters, which are themselves perhaps indifferently traced. This is one of the most fruitful sources of illegibility in longhand-writing, and should be seriously striven against by all who have fallen into the habit. If these letters are clearly distinguished, the others will be deciphered without much difficulty. It may be thought that a good and neat Shorthand writer will necessarily write a good and neat longhand. This is generally the case, but by no means invariably.

The indifferent writer should repress any tendency to write too rapidly—for legibility. If he can only write well by writing more slowly, he should write more slowly, unless speed is an urgent necessity. I have already referred to the desirability of neatness in shorthand transcripts of legal proceedings and other official work. Even if it were true, which it is not, that "anything will do for the printers," the dictum can never apply to documents of a quasi-official character, not perhaps intended for the printing office, but for ordinary use. I do not recommend the round school-boy style of the law-writer. Legible though it be, it is objectionable in its sameness and want of character. The ideal hand is one which combines both character and legibility. A good deal of the copy that finds its way to the printer is simply atrocious. It is an intricate collection of symbols, at which the editors, if they ever read it, are disgusted, and printers rebellious. Many a situation has been lost in consequence of careless writing; the inference not unnaturally drawn by employers being that a man who is careless in one thing will probably be careless in others. If manuscript copy has to undergo revision before going to the printers, there is still more need for legibility, and care should be taken to keep the lines sufficiently apart to admit of corrections and interlineations.

To those who find writing irksome, the use of the type-writer may be safely recommended. I have little doubt, indeed, that this useful instrument will gradually supersede, at any rate to a large extent, the use of the pen in connection with press work, as it is already doing in mercantile offices. I strongly recommend every young reporter to become a typist as well. Older hands may find it difficult to spare the necessary time to go through the needful drudgery. A few weeks' steady practice will enable a young man or woman to write with the type-writer almost, if not quite, as fast as an ordinary penman; and in a few months the penman's speed ought to be outstripped. I have had several trials with good typists, and, though a rapid longhand writer, have been unable to keep up with them. Very high speed has been obtained by some operators; but they should not be taken as specimens of what can be accomplished in ordinary practice. Short "spurts" are no more trustworthy guides of actual *practicable* speed in type-writing than they are in shorthand. They may be interesting as "records," but are of little value as tests of every day work. Sixty words a minute is an extremely good speed to be kept up for several hours continuously, and I have known few typists to exceed it. At this rate a column of the *Times* can be written in about forty minutes,—much more rapidly, that is, than a skilful penman can accomplish the task. Or, to use the familiar standard of the Shorthand writer, fifty "folios" may at the same rate be type-written in one hour, which greatly exceeds any ordinary transcript writing that I have seen or heard of in my own experience. In America, I believe that the type-writer is used in nearly all Shorthand writers' offices, and that transcripts written with the pen are almost unknown. The notetaker either transcribes his notes on the type-writer himself or dictates it to someone else, who either takes it in shorthand to be subsequently type-written, or (if he is a very rapid operator) follows the dictator directly on the machine without any stenographic intervention. These methods are adopted to some extent in a few English offices, but are by no means general. That they will become so, I think, is hardly to be doubted. The neatness and legibility of good type-writing are so attractive to most readers, that they will always prefer it to the best written manuscript. The machines are undoubtedly expensive, but they may become less so in time. One machine is of little use where there is any pressure of work; but with two or three working simultaneously, a vast amount of copy or transcript can be turned out in a few hours. It must be admitted that dictating to a typist is not the pleasantest occupation imaginable. The rattling of the keys is so noisy that the voice must be raised if the dictator is to be distinctly heard; and if this is continued for some hours the fatigue is considerable. That, at least, has been my own experience. If the operator is required to stop while a sentence is being dictated in a low tone of voice, so as to spare the exertion of the reader or dictator, time is lost, and the speed of the work reduced.

There are several machines in the market which will answer the purpose of the reporter and shorthand writer. I can only speak from experience of the Bar-Lock and the Remington, which do their work admirably. There are some cheap instruments fairly well adapted to slower type-writing, but I cannot recommend them for transcribing notes, a process in which speed is generally an important element. Both the Bar-Lock and the Remington, can be used advantageously for writing several copies at the same time, by the aid of carbonized paper and "flimsy." If only two copies are required, a much thicker paper can be used for the transcript; but as the number of copies is increased the thickness of the paper must be reduced. The ordinary printers' contractions may be used with the type-writer as with the pen. Some use *t* for "the" instead of a simple, / sloping stroke, and *tt* for "that." My own practice is to use for "the" the sloping stroke dividing shillings from pence. The slope does not agree with the upright type, but that is of very little consequence for printer's copy. It is perfectly legible, and it obviates the necessity of writing two *t's* for "that."

CHAPTER XXIII.

WRITING MATERIALS.

THE question of writing materials is one which deserves some special consideration at the hands of the Shorthand writer and reporter. The first question usually asked by a beginner is whether in note-taking he should use a pen or a pencil. The majority of newspaper reporters use pencils, but I have always recommended the use of a pen. A pencil has the convenience that it is a complete instrument in itself, and only requires occasional sharpening to keep it in order; but it has the serious disadvantage that its strokes are not permanent, and are considerably lighter than those made by a pen and ink, and cannot, therefore, be so easily read. Young men with good eyesight may not experience much difficulty in deciphering a pencil note, even by artificial light, but at a more advanced age the strain of such work, if long continued, is considerable, and should, if possible, be avoided. A good pen gives a well-defined stroke, distinguishing more easily than a pencil thick strokes from thin, and for these reasons most professional Shorthand writers, as distinguished from reporters, prefer to use a pen. Formerly, quill pens were employed by them, but now they are rarely, if ever, seen in a Shorthand writer's hands. Now that gold pens are plentiful and cheap, they are very frequently used for Shorthand purposes. I know no better implement than Mordan's guinea gold pen. It is expensive, but will with care last a lifetime. I used one for about thirty years, and should probably be using it still, if I had not had the misfortune to lose it. Fountain pens are also used for Shorthand writing with great advantage. It is sometimes inconvenient to have to use an inkstand at all, especially when writing on the knee, and the time lost in dipping is appreciable when following a rapid speaker. A fountain pen is thus a great desideratum in reporting. But it must be a good one. The ink must flow easily, but not too easily. If it becomes clogged and refuses to flow, or if it drops huge blots upon the note-book, it is worse than useless, the reporter's time being lost instead of saved, and the completeness of his note seriously imperilled. No pen should be trusted for a long report until it has been thoroughly tested. Messrs. Mabie, Todd and Bard's Fountain Pens are the best I have tried. But care should be taken in selecting a suitable one. The pen itself should be substantial, but rather fine-pointed and decidedly flexible. If it is "scratchy," it will be a source of endless annoyance. It should run smoothly over the paper and never miss fire, however rapid the writing. Different styles of writing require different pens; a light hand will need a finer pen than a heavier one. Each writer will soon ascertain by experience what pen suits him best. But no reporter or shorthand writer should rely upon a single pen: he should always have another pen or a pencil to fall back upon in case of need. If an accident happens to a pen, it is extremely inconvenient not to have another instrument to replace it. I have in my own experience known the nib of a pen to stick fast in the holder when the shorter part of the latter has been withdrawn from the longer part. Such an accident at the beginning of a speech is apt to be very disconcerting, and unless another pen or pencil is at hand the result may be the loss of many sentences. A pencil is preferable to a pen when writing in the dark. This is not an unknown experience to the reporter. He is occasionally required to take notes in rooms purposely darkened for exhibition purposes, where he cannot see a single stroke of his pen, and is even uncertain whether he has made a stroke or not. With a pencil he may be sure that he is writing something, but a pen may run dry without his knowing it. A pencil therefore should be used on such occasions. It is also preferable to a pen when standing and writing in the open air, as at a funeral. It is more easily manipulated than a pen, and in the event of rain the characters are not so much blurred by the drops as they are likely to be when written in ink.

As to ink, I have generally used Stephen's Blue Black, and have found it very serviceable. The same makers have another ink, styled Mixed Blue and Black, which is rather more flowing, and therefore specially suitable for the Fountain pen. Messrs. Pitman and Sons have lately introduced a new ink which is likely to answer extremely well for reporting purposes.

In regard to paper, I can only say that it should be hard and smooth, but not too highly glazed. A rather rough paper is suitable enough for a pencil but not for a pen.

Reporters' note-books may be had of all sizes and at all prices, from a penny to two shillings. The small ones are more convenient for the pocket, but they do not contain enough paper for a shorthand writer who is much engaged in note-taking. For the general run of shorthand work, a good sized book, say 7½ inches by 4½ and containing 120 leaves, is in my opinion the best. Such a book will suffice for a thousand folios of shorthand. It should be bound with india-rubber at the back, in order that the leaves may lie flat and turn over easily. If they are bound in sections in the ordinary way, the leaves bulge, and present an awkward surface to write upon. Many reporters write on unruled paper; but the advantage of writing on lines is very great, and every phonographer should certainly use them. The positions of the characters cannot be so well shown without them, and although they are not indispensable, they are of considerable assistance both in writing and in reading. In my own practice I have always used double lines, which, however, Mr. Pitman does not recommend They are more troublesome to obtain, as all stationers dc not keep them in stock; but I think they afford a decided advantage in enabling the writer to distinguish consonants in the first position (beginning as they do above the top line and coming through it), and to keep the writing within moderate dimensions, checking the tendency to make the characters unnecessarily large when following a rapid speaker. I am aware that the great majority of phonographers use single lines. Whichever plan is adopted, the lines of writing should not be too close; they should be sufficiently wide apart to prevent the writing on one line coming in contact with that on the line above or below. As to the use of interleaved blotting paper, I can only say that I see no necessity for it, except in the case of very heavy writers, whose writing is likely on turning over a leaf to blot the one on which it falls. But a single leaf of blotting paper at the beginning and end of the book will be found convenient for occasional use.

Before leaving the subject of note-books, let me recommend every reporter to make a practice of keeping his books and indexing their contents. He can never tell when he may be called upon to produce them, and perhaps to supply transcripts of what he has written, which of course bring grist to the mill. It is the custom of legal Shorthand writers to index all their cases inside the covers of their note-books for future reference. This is more needful in their case than in the case of the newspaper reporter; but the practice will be found serviceable in both branches of the Shorthand profession. I have myself been called upon to produce in Court notes taken more than twenty years previously, and while writing these pages I have received instructions to transcribe some notes taken more than thirty years ago.

There are many kinds of reporters' inkstands from which a selection may be made. For writing on a table, the inkstand should have a firm base, so as not to be easily upset. A rather large and heavy inkstand is the best for writing purposes; but it is inconvenient for carrying in the pocket. For writing on the knee, nothing is better than the common excise inkstand, which can be held in the left hand, or allowed to hang over the back of the hand by means of an elastic band fastened round the neck of the bottle, leaving a sufficient loop to go round the hand. The latter method has the advantage of leaving the fingers free to manipulate the leaves of the note-book. For sermon reporting and other occasions when no table or desk is available, this is a matter of some importance.

CHAPTER XXIV.

SHORTHAND FOR THE LEARNED PROFESSIONS.

MY little book would hardly be complete without some reference to the uses of Shorthand in connection with the learned and other professions in which the pen is constantly called into requisition. In view of the obvious advantages which the art offers to clergymen, lawyers, and doctors, it might almost be expected that it would form a necessary part of the curriculum of students destined for those professions, since it is a valuable instrument, not merely in the acquisition of knowledge, but in its application to the purposes of professional life. I have known, and still know, distinguished members of the three great professions, who have frankly and gratefully owned that much of the success which they have achieved has been attributable to their early practice and continued use of Shorthand.

To the student, in any profession, it is not easy to overestimate the value of a simple and easy method of taking notes of college lectures, making extracts, and the like; while, for the purposes of original composition, a ready means of expression, such as Shorthand supplies, is an aid to study, which no one, who has once acquired it, would willingly forego. In taking notes of lectures, however, the student should be recommended to use his Shorthand judiciously, and not encumber his note-book with verbatim reports when fairly copious summaries would suffice. Full reports should only be taken of lectures of the highest importance, and containing matter not easily obtainable from the text-books. To wade through a mass of Shorthand notes, and select a few salient points which may be serviceable at an examination, is a sheer waste of time; and, when the lectures are numerous, as in the medical schools, such a method of note-taking is almost impracticable. Some persons, indeed, have rather discouraged the use of Shorthand in student life, on the very ground that students are apt to over-use it, and to rely more upon their notes than upon their memories and their judgment. As among young reporters, so among students: there are those who use Shorthand mechanically, and not intelligently; but that, surely, is no reason for not using it at all. The best method of dealing with a course of lectures, for educational purposes, is to preserve a good summary of them for future reference; and this can be done much more easily and clearly in Shorthand than in longhand, leaving the student more at ease to listen to the parts of the teaching which he does not think it necessary to record. But, should he prefer to take full notes throughout, he should at least take the precaution to mark the important passages, so that, in making a summary afterwards, or in referring to the notes for other purposes, he may not be compelled to look through twenty or thirty pages in search of material that might be compressed into three or four.

For making extracts, notes of cases (medical and legal), and general references, the use of Shorthand to the student is hardly less important than its application to the purposes of taking down lectures. The saving of time is so considerable, that the student is enabled to make much more extensive notes than would be possible with longhand, or to devote more time to other branches of his work. The note-books should, of course, be kept and carefully indexed, and the writing should be neat and legible, in order that no difficulty may be experienced in deciphering it in after years. Much of it, no doubt, will never be referred to after the student days are over; but, it is impossible to say how useful and interesting a good collection of notes, made at a time when the mind is actively assimilating, may prove. Even if the information acquired be superseded or modified by later developments, the notes will have an historical interest which no real student can fail to appreciate.

Of the uses of Shorthand in actual professional life, ample illustrations may be given in connection with each of the three professions to which I have referred. To the clergyman who is in the habit of writing his sermons, Shorthand offers an obvious and direct method of saving many hours in every week, which are thus liberated for other work. If only half the mechanical labour of writing, say, two sermons weekly is saved—a low estimate even in the case of an indifferent writer of Shorthand—the amount of time thus set free in a single year may be reckoned by weeks, without taking into account the saving effected by the other uses of Shorthand for private memoranda and note-taking in connection with professional studies. For sermon or lecture writing, as for any kind of writing which is to be read in public, it is of the first importance that a clear, legible style be cultivated. A slovenly manuscript may lead to unpleasant hesitations; but many besides myself can testify from personal experience that a clearly written Shorthand manuscript is quite as easy to read from as longhand. Indeed, I am disposed to think that it is easier. The letters and words being grouped more closely together, the eye takes them in with greater ease; and, if phraseography be judiciously used, space is saved, an entire sentence is seized at a glance, and the reader need not constantly keep his eye on the written page. The feeling and appearance of constraint are thus lessened, to the manifest advantage both of the reader and the listener. If the writing is fairly large and distinct, and catch-words are plainly underlined, the reading is rendered all the easier, and the words can be uttered almost with the freedom and naturalness of extemporaneous speech.

The special use of Shorthand to the medical man in his daily practice is in making notes of cases that come under his observation and treatment, whether in the hospital or in private practice. I have known several physicians, good phonographers, whose habit it has been, when visiting a patient, to jot down in their note-books the results of their inquiries, for reference, if required, at subsequent visits; and they have told me that they have found the practice to be one of great convenience and utility. But for this aid, many little details, at first apparently insignificant, but assuming importance later on, might be forgotten. A medical practitioner often sees a large number of patients daily, and, however good his memory, he can hardly be expected to remember every detail of each patient's complaints. A Shorthand diary would bring everything back to his recollection, and assist him in his diagnosis and treatment.

To the lawyer, of either branch of the profession, but especially to the barrister, a practical knowledge of Shorthand presents advantages which it offers to few other men. Solicitors, it is true, in large practice are now accustomed to delegate most of their writing to Shorthand clerks; but this is a luxury generally denied to the barrister. He may, indeed, dictate his opinions in his chambers; but, when engaged in a case in Court, he must be his own scribe. If he has attained the position of a leader, he may leave most of the note-taking to his junior; but often, when listening to the evidence of a witness, or a speech to which he has to reply, he finds it convenient and even necessary to make a note of the "points" with which he has to deal; and, if he can do this in Shorthand, he will do it more easily and with greater exactitude. In a long case, with many witnesses, it is not uncommon to see a junior laboriously writing down, day after day, on the backs of the sheets of his brief, all the evidence given throughout the trial. He might save himself much of this toil, and secure a more perfect note, if he wrote in Shorthand. Some barristers, appreciating the advantage of this method of saving time, have learned and practised Shorthand, and may often be seen in Court taking down evidence with much less effort than their brethren not similarly qualified. The time wasted in legal trials while evidence is being slowly taken down by the Judge, is almost a scandal in judicial proceedings in this country, as in many others. A few judges have learned Shorthand, and turned it to practical use on the Bench. But these instances are rare; and, unless professional Shorthand writers are engaged, so as to relieve the Judge of the necessity of minute note-taking, the cases drag their slow length along, to the vexation of the client and the waste of an enormous amount of public time and expense.

These may be taken as typical examples of the value of Shorthand in professional life. They might be multiplied indefinitely by a reference to the other professions—those of the architect, the surveyor, the engineer, the electrician, and the like. Even the artist and the musician might, occasionally, with advantage, express themselves in Shorthand. Its use has already been recommended in high quarters in connection with the profession of arms, as affording the means of rapid communication on the field and elsewhere. In brief, wherever writing is needed, as it now is in almost every calling in life, Shorthand steps in, and offers its services in substitution for the clumsy longhand, which, notwithstanding its services in the past, is utterly inadequate to meet the requirements of to-day.

CHAPTER XXV.

LIBEL.

ONE of the inconveniences and perils of the journalist is his liability to actions for libel. Many such actions are brought every year, and damages are often recovered for injuries that are purely imaginary. Unscrupulous solicitors have a quick eye for anything that may be construed into a libellous statement; and many a paragraph, written with the most innocent intention, has been followed by a writ, and the writer or publisher mulcted in a heavy penalty or even committed to prison. It might be supposed that a reporter need have no apprehension on this score so long as he faithfully recorded the words of the speakers whom he was called upon to report; that is, that he might shift the responsibility of any calumnious statement on to the shoulders of the speaker himself. This, however, is only partially true, and it is important that the reporter should understand how far his exemption from liability extends. (I am not, of course, speaking of his personal liability, but of that of his employer, the proprietor or publisher of the journal on which he is engaged.) Formerly, if an action for libel was brought against a newspaper for the publication of a libellous statement occurring, say, in the report of a public meeting, it was no answer to say that the report was an accurate one and was published without malice. Judges were in the habit of pointing out that such a liberty of publication would be dangerous, because it would be easy to hold a public meeting for the express purpose of uttering defamatory statements, and then to throw the responsibility of publishing them upon the papers in which they were reported. This has been somewhat modified of late years, and the present state of the law is, in regard to the privileges attaching to newspaper reports, to be found in the Law of Libel Amendment Act, 1888. By that Act (Sec. 3) a fair and accurate report in any newspaper of proceedings publicly heard before any Court exercising judicial authority "shall, if published contemporaneously with such proceedings, be privileged: provided that nothing in this section shall authorize the publication of any blasphemous or indecent matter." The privilege, it will be seen, is taken away if the report be not fair and accurate, if the proceedings be not public, or if any of the reported matter be blasphemous or indecent. In regard to public meetings and statutory bodies, the privilege and its limitations are defined in Section 4, which every journalist should know by heart:—

"A fair and accurate report published in any newspaper of the proceedings of a public meeting, or (except where neither the public nor any newspaper reporter is admitted) of any meeting of a vestry, town council, school board, board of guardians, board or local authority formed or constituted under the provisions of any Act of Parliament, or of any committee appointed by any of the above-mentioned bodies, or of any meeting of any commissioners authorised to act by letters patent, Act of Parliament, warrant under the Royal Sign Manual, or other lawful warrant or authority, select committees of either House of Parliament, justices of the peace in quarter sessions assembled for administrative or deliberative purposes, and the publication at the request of any Government office or department, officer of state, commissioner of police, or chief constable of any notice or report issued by them for the information of the public, shall be privileged, unless it shall be proved that such report or publication was published or made maliciously: Provided that nothing in this section shall authorize the publication of any blasphemous or indecent matter: Provided also, that the protection intended to be afforded by this section shall not be available as a defence in any proceedings if it shall be proved that the defendant has been requested to insert in the newspaper in which the report or other publication complained of appeared, a reasonable letter or statement by way of contradiction or explanation of such report or other publication, and has refused or neglected to insert the same: Provided further, that nothing in this section contained shall be deemed or construed to limit or abridge any privilege now by law existing, or to protect the publication of any matter not of public concern and the publication of which is not for the public benefit."

For the purposes of this section a "public" meeting is defined to be:—"Any meeting *bonâ fide* and lawfully held for a lawful purpose, and for the furtherance or discussion of any matter of public concern, whether the admission thereto be general or restricted."

In view of these provisions, if for no other reason, it is obvious that great care should be taken in reporting matter that is, or may be taken to be, of a libellous character. In the first place, the report should be fair and accurate. This is especially the case in regard to law proceedings. There should not be even the appearance of partiality. If the plaintiff's case is fully reported, the defendant's should not be unduly abridged; and no documents should be printed that have not been read in Court. The neglect of this latter precaution has occasionally led newspapers into trouble. In one case a document was lent to a reporter, who reproduced portions of it that had never been read at the trial; and as these contained matter that was held to be libellous, the newspaper had to pay considerable damages. Special care should be given in reporting names. Actions have sometimes been brought in consequence of wrong initials. Inadvertences of this kind are readily seized upon by lynx-eyed solicitors, and severe penalties are sometimes exacted. Many cases of the kind have to be compromised, and never come before the public.

It is not easy to say what constitutes a libel. It has been defined to be anything calculated to bring a man into contempt. The late Baron Huddleston gave it a still wider definition: "Anything likely to disparage a man." If this were strictly acted upon, every disparaging observation in a newspaper might be the subject of an action. A great deal of latitude is always allowed in comments on a man's public career; but animadversions on his personal character, imputations upon his honesty and respectability, are on a different footing, and the reporter should hesitate before giving such statements to the public, or should at least call the attention of the editor to them, in order to relieve himself from responsibility in the matter. It is true that a certain protection is now given to reports at public meetings; but not only must the meetings be of the character defined by the Act, but the matter reported must be "of public concern," and not mere private abuse. Nor should it be forgotten that companies and commercial firms as well as private individuals may be the subjects of a libel, and any remarks calculated to injure their credit can only be published at great risk.

Criminal prosecutions for libel are now comparatively rare, one reason being that they cannot be instituted without an order of a Judge at Chambers; and they rarely succeed unless great malice is proved on the part of the offending paper.

CHAPTER XXVI.

BOOKS OF REFERENCE.

NOTHING in the way of material stock-in-trade is more valuable to the reporter or Shorthand writer than a good reference library; and I strongly recommend every young man (or woman) who intends to pursue either branch of the profession, to begin collecting in his very earliest days. His odd shillings will be much better spent in books than in cigars; and the satisfaction of seeing his shelves gradually filled with volumes that will not only be useful to him as a student, but will serve his purpose in professional life, will be ample compensation for any little sacrifice that he may make in order to accomplish his object. A reporter without a little reference library of his own will be constantly at a loss. I know that he may have access to many such libraries far larger than any that he can hope to collect for himself: but he is not always in a position to visit them, and the more independent he can be of their aid the better. To the Londoner the grand store-house of knowledge of every kind, so far as books can convey it, is, of course, the British Museum, and everyone who can obtain a reading order—no difficult matter now-a-days—should do so. Every new book published in the United Kingdom finds it way to this superb National collection, which also contains an abundant supply of ancient and mediæval works in all languages. Dictionaries, Gazetteers, Biographies, Concordances, Encyclopædias and the like, crowd the vast shelves of the noble reading-room, and can be removed and consulted by the visitor without the slightest trouble; and such works as are not on the shelves can be written for on slips of paper, and will be brought by the attendants to the readers' desk, where pens and ink are provided for his use. Amidst the enormous profusion that surrounds him he may, if not an habitué, be occasionally puzzled in the pursuit of his investigations; but the attendants are always ready and pleased to put him on the right track, and he is made to feel that the whole resources of the establishment are at his disposal. But it is not everyone, even in London, who can often make it convenient to visit the British Museum to turn up a name, or a date, or a quotation. Happily, however, there are both in London and in the Provinces other libraries easily accessible to the public, in which good works of reference are to be found. The Guildhall Library, for example, is open to the public without any order, and is well-supplied with books of almost every description. Another Library which is but little known, is that attached to the Patent Office, and situated between Southampton Buildings and Quality Court, Chancery Lane. To a reporter or shorthand writer it is of great value, containing as it does a splendid collection of books on every branch of science and art, including the best encyclopædias, dictionaries of technical terms in various languages, law reports, and other useful works of reference. It is also provided with many of the English and foreign technical journals as they are published. It is open daily to the public without restriction, and every assistance is cheerfully rendered by the attendants. I have already mentioned that the Institute of Shorthand Writers has a good library of the Law Reports and other works that are so often cited in legal proceedings; but the use of this is limited to its own members. I have also noticed the Gallery Library, accessible only to Parliamentary reporters. The Institute of Journalists has no reference library for the use of its members; but this is a desideratum that may yet be supplied. There are splendid libraries in connection with the Inns of Court, in which all legal works of reference and many others may be found; but these are not open to the public, and an introduction is needed before permission is given to consult them. I have said nothing of subscription libraries. If the reporter can afford to subscribe to Mudie's or any other large library of its class, he will find it an advantage not only for his own private reading, but for obtaining books from which to verify quotations occuring in his notes. Libraries of this kind, however, are not of much service in the way of ordinary books of reference,—Dictionaries, Gazetteers, &c.

Among the books of reference with which a reporter should provide himself, one of the first is, of course, a good English dictionary. I suppose no one, however well informed he may be, can afford to dispense with such aid. To say nothing of the meanings of words, especially unfamiliar ones, their orthography is a matter of so much uncertainty as to necessitate an occasional appeal to a dictionary. It is true that these authorities differ in not a few instances, and in such cases, the writer must exercise his own discretion. If he is a Phonographer, his phonetic instinct or habit will lead him to write *program* instead of *programme*, and to drop superfluous letters whenever the omission is permitted by any respectable authority. It may be that his spelling will not be adopted by the printers, who will prefer to follow the rules of their respective offices; but in some cases, he may be able to establish his own standard. In regard to the meanings of words, the reporter, like every other contributor to the press, needs the friendly aid of the dictionary. He should never transcribe a word of which he does not know the meaning, without turning it up for his enlightenment. Even in his ordinary reading, an unknown word should not be allowed to pass without a reference to the dictionary. He may meet with it in his own note-taking, and may be perplexed if he fails to recognize it. When, many years ago, I first saw the word "altruism," I made a mental note of it and its signification. The very next day it occurred in a speech that I was reporting, and as the speaker was very indistinct, I have little doubt that it would have escaped me, but for the previous day's experience. Many words of very different meaning are so similar in sound that it is very easy to mistake them; and this is the source of many of the reporter's errors with which men of education sometimes make merry. A reporter, for example, who has never met with the word "hedonism" is very likely to write it "heathenism"; and I have more than once seen "immanent" rendered "imminent." The moral of all this is, that the reporter should, as a matter of professional precaution, be *on the look out for unfamiliar words*, and endeavour to memorize them. If he is only a moderately diligent reader, and is wise enough to give a wide range to the subjects of his reading, he will be sure to meet with new words which may some day find their way into his note-book, and it will conduce greatly to his comfort if he can recognize them as old acquaintances. Few persons, perhaps, care to while away an hour by reading a dictionary; yet, a good deal of instruction, if not of entertainment, may be gained in this way. It is, undoubtedly, a humiliating experience, revealing an amount of ignorance on the part of the reader which possibly he had not suspected; but the revelation will have its uses if it only gives an insight into new subjects and awakens the slightest interest in them. A good illustrated dictionary is, in reality, one of the most readable of books. The Phonographer can even extract amusement from the most forbidding of polysyllables by devising and practising good shorthand outlines for their expression: an exercise that will serve to fix the words in his memory. It will often be found that a difficult word, a long foreign name for example, which cannot be easily recalled, although it has been seen in print and heard, will, if it be associated with a shorthand outline, readily recur to the mind. The phonographic forms have a distinctive character of their own, which can hardly be said of words printed in the common type, and their image is called up in such a way as to suggest at once the group of sounds presented.

One of the best and most comprehensive English dictionaries is the "Imperial" in four volumes (Ogilvie). It is well illustrated, and includes a great number of technical terms not to be found in smaller lexicons. It has an excellent Appendix containing a pronouncing vocabulary of Greek, Latin, scriptural and other ancient names; a similar vocabulary of modern geographical names, lists of foreign words and phrases met with in current English, and of abbreviations and contractions commonly used in writing and printing. Webster's Dictionary in one volume (Bell and Sons) is another extremely useful work of reference suitable for a reporter's library. The last edition is well up to date, containing scientific and other terms of recent origin. It has also a very serviceable list of characters in fiction, whose names so often find their way into speeches as well as into other kinds of literary composition—names with which the reporter, if not extremely well read, may not always be familiar. Perhaps the most extensive English Dictionary is "The Century," in six large volumes (T. Fisher Unwin.) Like Webster's, it is of American origin, and is a marvel of industrious compilation. I can hardly include in my list the great dictionary of Dr. Murray now in preparation at

Oxford, since it has only dealt with a few letters of the alphabet. When it is finished it will, no doubt, be the most complete work of its kind ever published. It traces the history of every word, giving illustrations of its varied meanings, changes, and spellings. It will be a costly work, but it should be on the shelves of every literary man who can afford the outlay.

As to foreign dictionaries, they will be of little service to the reporter unless he knows something of the languages of which they are the repositories. A Latin and a French dictionary will probably be most frequently needed. To those who are in the habit of reporting sermons, a Greek Lexicon and a Greek Testament are almost indispensable. Some preachers make frequent references to the original Greek text, and the reporter should always be able to verify them.

Among encyclopædias nothing can approach "The Encyclopædia Britannica," either for fulness or accuracy; but it is too costly for most persons. "Chambers's Encyclopædia" is a much smaller work, but it is very complete as far as it goes, and I have rarely consulted it in vain. "Blackie's Modern Cyclopædia" is also a very useful work.

The aid of a Gazetteer is often needed by the reporter. "The Imperial" (Blackie) is an excellent one; and "The General Dictionary of Geography," by A. Keith Johnston, may be safely recommended.

A good Biographical Dictionary is another useful addition to a library. "The National" is not completed; but, like Dr. Murray's Dictionary, it is very perfect as far as it has gone, and will in the end prove a most comprehensive storehouse of biographical information. "The Imperial" (Mackenzie) is one of the best completed works, but it is rather expensive. I may also mention the "Dictionary of Biographical Reference," containing a hundred thousand names, with references to dictionaries and other works where fuller accounts of each individual may be found.

For sermon reporting "Cruden's Concordance" is indispensable, and a copy of the large edition (the abridged editions are of little value) can be obtained for a few shillings. But the sermon reporter should remember that a scriptural quotation cannot always be discovered by a reference to Cruden. The parliamentary reporters were once terribly puzzled with a citation by the Duke of Argyll: "The Lord reigneth, be the people never so impatient." He followed it up by declaring that the people were impatient, and the quotation was therefore important in a full report. But it could not be found in Cruden or in the Bible, and, not liking to run any risk, the reporters omitted the passage and the succeeding comment. They afterwards ascertained that the quotation was from the Prayer-book version of the Psalms, which often differs from the Authorized Version. (A Concordance to the Prayer-book, including the Psalms, is published by the Society for the Promotion of Christian Knowledge.) It is as well, too, to remember that some preachers habitually use the Revised Version both for their texts and their quotations; while others, like the late Canon Liddon, prefer to give renderings of their own, differing from both the received versions. Sometimes it will be found that a verse is quoted from the Apocrypha, to which a separate division of Cruden is devoted.

Among the miscellaneous books of reference I may mention "Haydn's Dictionary of Dates," the "Technological Dictionary," English, French and German (Samson, Low, & Co.), "McCulloch's Commercial Dictionary," (Longmans), a "Dictionary of Science and Technical Terms," by W. M. Buchanan, (W. Tegg and Co.), and "Adeline's Art Dictionary," an index of terms used in art, architecture, heraldry and archæology, (Virtue). Most of the words to be found in these volumes are included in the larger general dictionaries; but the explanations in the latter are, of course, much less complete.

For classical names, "Smith's Classical Dictionary," (Murray) is the best for general use. Lemprière is now quite out of date. Bohn's "Dictionary of Classical Quotations" is a valuable book for the reporter; not perhaps so essential as in former days, when many statesmen interlarded their speeches with Latin and Greek, but still serviceable for occasional reference.

For all kinds of official information "Whitaker's Almanac" can generally be consulted with advantage. "Dod's Parliamentary Companion" gives the names of all the members of both Houses of Parliament. "Hazell's Encyclopædia" (annual) is another compendium of useful information.

"Roget's Thesaurus" (Longmans) is a list of words and phrases, classified and arranged "so as to facilitate the expression of ideas and assist in literary composition." It is, in fact, a dictionary of synonyms, and will often help the reporter who is at a loss for a suitable word to express his meaning or the meaning of a speaker whom he is reporting.

For poetical quotations the reporter has generally to consult the authors themselves. Shakesperian citations can always be found by a reference to Mrs. Cowden Clarke's Concordance; and there is also a concordance to Tennyson which will facilitate a search for any of the Poet Laureate's lines. Shakespere, Milton and Tennyson should be on the reporter's shelves, and if he can purchase, say the Aldine Edition of the British poets, they will amply repay the outlay. "Familiar Quotations," too, may be serviceable to the reporter, if only to enable him to correct some of the common misquotations into which many speakers are betrayed.

CHAPTER XXVII.

COMPOSITION.

A GOOD style of composition is as essential to a reporter as it is to an author; and this not only for descriptive work, but for the transcription of shorthand notes of public speeches. I am not suggesting that the reporter should be, in point of style, a Gibbon, or a Macaulay, or a Froude. But he should at least be able to write good grammatical English, and express himself clearly, and, when needful, forcibly; I would even add eloquently, but for the fear of being misunderstood. I have already uttered a warning against fine writing; but I have nothing to say against an elegant style, as properly understood; that is, a clear, smooth, graceful, bright, and crisp method of expression, free from every taint of vulgarism on the one hand and of inflation on the other. To some this seems to come by instinct. We read the easy and flowing sentences, and imagine that they have been penned with the utmost ease and spontaneity. The inference may be a wholly mistaken one. The very passage that appears so simply and delightfully constructed may be the one which has been subjected to the severest scrutiny and revision. Its very simplicity is a masterpiece of art, effectually concealing the labor which has been bestowed upon it (*ars celare artem*). Excellence in this direction can hardly be acquired in the absence of the natural gift; nor is it attained, except, perhaps, in very rare instances, without patient study and diligent practice. *Le style, c'est l'homme*, said Buffon; and no one has more happily illustrated the dictum than the great naturalist himself.

I have no right, and certainly no desire, to assume the office of instructor in the matter of composition and style; and if I offer a few hints on the subject, it is only with a view of securing for it the attention which it deserves from my younger readers, and leading them to consult other authorities and study other models, by whose aid they may correct the careless and slipshod style of expression so common to the untrained and imperfectly educated scribe.

The first essential of composition is, of course, clearness. And clearness depends, first, on the use of appropriate words. This is so obvious a consideration that it needs no enforcement. No word should be used the exact signification of which is not understood by the writer. I do not mean that its etymology should invariably be known and appreciated. Etymology, useful as it may be, and often is, in determining the propriety of using a particular word, is not always a guide to its ordinary and accepted meaning. Words, it has been well said, often drift from their moorings; that is, they may come to have a wider or a narrower signification than the words from which they have been derived, or may even come to express entirely different ideas. It would be absurd and pedantic to use such words in their original sense. To "prevent," according to its Latin equivalent, is to *go before*, to *anticipate* ("Prevent us, O Lord, in all our doings"); but it now means to obstruct, and it would be simply affectation to use it in any other way. "Insolent," in its Latin form, means *unusual, unaccustomed;* yet we should hardly say that a lady smoking a cigar was acting insolently. A "miscreant" was formerly used to signify, according to its etymology, a *misbeliever;* but no one would now dream of using it in that sense. In many cases, however, the knowledge of the derivation of a word may be serviceable in preventing an unfortunate or inappropriate use of it. The word "decimate" refers to the practice of punishing every tenth man in a regiment; and it is, therefore, hardly suitable, though it is sometimes used, to express almost entire annihilation. But its use has certainly been enlarged. Webster gives as its secondary meaning, "To destroy a considerable part of." The misuse of the word "mutual," instead of "common," as in the phrase "a mutual friend," has been so often pointed out that any further reference to it might be considered unnecessary. But the practice still lingers, and I therefore cite it as an example of careless writing or speaking. The word "mutual," of course, implies *reciprocity* or *interchange*, and is not applicable to anything that is *common* to two or more persons or things. "Reliable" has its apologists, but I agree with Mr. Lowell in thinking it abominable. "Dependable" is still worse. "Talented" has been denounced as a barbarism, but it is used by good writers. "Different to" is often wrongly used for "different from." Sometimes "than" is made to follow "different," as "It is very different learning a language without any assistance from a teacher or a companion than it is when you are in the country itself." When, as in this case, "than" follows at some distance from "different," its want of accord may possibly be overlooked; but it is none the less a mistake which should be corrected. "*From* what it is" (instead of "*than* it is") may not be elegant, but it is better than using "different—than." Of course, the sentence would be better reconstructed thus:—"Learning a language without the assistance of a teacher or companion is very different from learning it in the country in which it is spoken."

The employment of foreign words, unless their signification and their grammatical relations are well understood, is very perilous to the writer. It is very common to see the word "exposé" used in the sense of exposure, its true meaning being simply an exposition, a setting forth. A writer ignorant of French will write "protégé," or "employé," though it may apply to a female, not knowing that an additional "e" is required for the feminine form of the word. I have often seen "bona fides" (good faith) written with a circumflex over the "a," the writer having, no doubt, been misled by seeing it so used in "bonâ fide" (in good faith), where, to indicate the ablative case, the circumflex is needed. The most elementary knowledge of the Latin grammar would have prevented the mistake. A young reporter, whose knowledge of Latin was limited to some dozen or two phrases in c mmon use, in the course of a descriptive paragraph wrote:—"It is a case not of *rus in urbe*, but of *urbe in rus*." Knowing that *rus in urbe* meant "country in town," he rashly came to the conclusion—and perhaps prided himself on the antithesis—that *urbe in rus* was the proper form for "town in country," never dreaming that it should be written "urbs in rure." The plurals in foreign words often trip up the unwary. I have frequently seen and heard "strata" and "phenomena" used in the singular. One living lady orator, whom I have often reported, constantly speaks of "this wonderful phenomena."

Next in importance to the selection of appropriate words comes their judicious arrangement. The careful reporter, when transcribing his notes, constantly finds it necessary, in order to avoid ambiguity, to change the position of a word or phrase. He may not have occasion to alter a single word in the sentence; a simple transposition is all that is required. A speaker says:—"The Secretary of State has brought forward a measure which will destroy the prosperity of the country in the very last year of his tenure of office." This implies that the prosperity of the country will be destroyed in the last year of his tenure of office; but what is meant by the speaker is that in the last year of his office the Secretary of State brought forward a measure, etc.; and this is clearly expressed by placing the words, "In the very last year," etc., either at the commencement of the sentence or after the words, "The Secretary of State." A public speaker can hardly be expected to avoid slips of this kind, and the error is, perhaps, one of the commonest that a reporter has to correct. The speaker himself may by tone and emphasis render the words perfectly intelligible; but as tone and emphasis are not transferred to the written or the printed page, the reader is more liable to be misled than were the listeners. Sometimes the effect of an ill-arranged collocation of words is ludicrous in the extreme, as the pages of *Punch* abundantly testify. It is not often that one meets with so peculiar a sentence as "Wanted, a young man to take care of a horse of the Methodist persuasion"; or as, "A whale was harpooned by a sailor weighing twenty-five tons"; or (perhaps still more remarkable) "He purchased a piano the property of a lady about to travel in an ebony case with carved legs." Punctuation may do something, in such cases, to remove ambiguity; but it hardly obviates the necessity for a re-arrangement of clauses.

As an instance of words that are often misplaced, I may cite "not only."' In my own practice I have found few words that more frequently need transposition. A speaker will say, "The hon. member not only spoke against the resolution, but against the amendment." What he means is, "The hon. member spoke not only against the resolution, but against the amendment." The words "not only spoke" suggest that the hon. member did something else, as, for example, "not only *spoke* against the resolution, but *voted* against it." Or a speaker may say, "The Prime Minister not only attended the meeting, but many of his followers accompanied him," really meaning, however, "Not only did the Prime Minister attend the meeting, but," etc. The first form suggests that the Prime Minister not only *attended* the meeting, but (for example) *spoke* at it. These may seem in themselves small matters, but they deserve careful attention. If the reporter, while transcribing his notes, uses his critical faculty in detecting and amending errors of this description, he will not only be conferring an obligation upon the speakers whom he reports, but will be improving his own style of original composition.

Some speakers and writers are obscure in consequence of an unwillingness to repeat a word once or twice in the same sentence. The frequent repetition of a word is not always agreeable, but it is preferable to ambiguity. A pronoun should never be used if there is any doubt as to its antecedent. Yet many writers will use "he" and "it" in sentences where there are several nouns to which these words might apply. "The word *it*," says Cobbett in his "Grammar," "is the greatest troubler I know of in language. Never put *it* upon paper without thinking well of what you are about. When I see many *its* in a page, I always tremble for the writer." Macaulay, who was a model of clearness, never hesitated to repeat a word as often as it might be needed to render the sentence intelligible.

Nor is clearness the only characteristic which is secured by a suitable arrangement of words and phrases. Force of expression, also, is often dependent upon the order in which words are written or spoken. This is especially noticeable in reference to the position of a conditional clause in a sentence. As a rule, such a clause should come at the beginning, and not at the end, where it is weak and flat. Take the sentence:—"He would not have died of the disorder from which he and many of his family suffered so much, if he had taken my advice." Change the position of the clause, "If he had taken my advice," to the beginning of the sentence, and the effect is greatly improved. The longer the sentence the greater the necessity for the conditional, or, as it has been called, the "if" clause being placed before the more material words. The reader or listener should be kept in suspense till the sentence is completed and the climax reached. This, no doubt, may be carried to an extreme, but, used judiciously, the principle of suspense in composition is decidedly effective, and its violation produces weakness and tameness. "Except ye repent, ye shall all likewise perish" is much more forcible than "Ye shall all likewise perish except ye repent." And, as Dr. Abbott says, everyone can see the flatness of "Revenge thy father's foul and most unnatural murder, if thou didst ever love him," as compared with "If ever thou didst thy dear father love, revenge his foul and most unnatural murder."

A very common fault in composition is redundancy. A reporter, whose duty it constantly is to expunge the needless verbiage of others, should never himself indulge in pleonasms. They may occasionally be excused on the ground of emphasis, but their general tendency is to weaken rather than to strengthen the sentences in which they are used. Such a sentence as "They all, without exception, unanimously declared," may at first sight seem emphatic; but in reality the words convey no more than the three words, "They all declared." It is often amusing to listen to a speaker returning thanks for a toast and to notice the redundancy of his words. He not only expresses his thanks, but his grateful thanks; that is, his thankful thanks. I have even heard, "My most cordial, heartfelt, and grateful thanks." The only difference between "cordial" and "heartfelt" is that the one is Latin and the other Saxon. A very objectionable pleonasm is "equally as"—equally as much, equally as great; but it is frequently met with in speech and in print. One often sees the words "mutually" and "each other" needlessly employed in the same sentence, as "they mutually helped each other." "Mutually" adds nothing to the meaning or force of the sentence, and is sheer waste. When a speaker says he has "finished it all," he uses three words when two would suffice. These are obvious instances which every reporter should at once detect and rectify. Others may not be so apparent. A reporter might easily transcribe "No credence should be given to the truth of the report," without observing that the words "the truth of" are entirely superfluous. I remember a judge (the late Lord Justice Knight-Bruce), who was a purist in such matters, calling a barrister (who afterwards sat on the bench with him) to task for saying, "It was one of the most unanimous meetings ever held." "How," said the learned judge, "could it be more than unanimous?" Such a phrase as "the reason for his so acting was because he wanted to secure his election," illustrates another common error in speaking and writing. The word "because" is a redundancy. "The reason . . . . . was that he wanted," etc., is the proper form. If "because" is retained, "reason" is redundant, and the wording should be, "He so acted because he wanted," etc.

The use of metaphorical language is another source of danger to the inexperienced or careless writer. "The hon. member never opens his mouth without putting his foot in it," is a characteristic illustration of the absurdities arising from mixed metaphors. I once heard, in India, an eloquent native orator declare:—"We knocked at the door of the House of Commons until we were hoarse." An Irish member (Sir Boyle Roche) is credited with the following:—"Mr. Speaker, I smell a rat; I see him brewing in the air. But, mark me, I shall yet nip him in the bud." Another sentence taken from a sermon is equally mixed:—"Walk up and down this little place till wicked men and dying women, lost in the desert, get saved from shipwreck and sail safe into the vineyard for evermore."

Exaggeration is another common fault of beginners. When employed humorously, it may be tolerated; but in ordinary writing the free use of superlatives is highly objectionable. "Most extraordinary," "immeasurably surpassing," "beyond all possible conception," and similar phrases, not only are in most cases inappropriate, but, by the frequency of their occurrence, lose their force, and are no longer effective when applied to the few cases in which they may be reasonably used. They are like the exaggerated emphasis of a speaker, unrelieved by lighter tones, fatiguing the listener, and giving no opportunity for real emphasis when it is needed. Here is a specimen that may be held up as a solemn warning to the young reporter:—"The entertainment was arranged with a *magnificence* that was perfectly *stupendous* and *most unprecedented*, and which quite kept up his lordship's *unrivalled* reputation for *unparalleled* hospitality, and, thanks to the *unequalled* energy of Mr. Smith, who is rapidly becoming one of the *most effective* toast-masters in the kingdom, the toasts were given with a spirit *quite unexampled* on occasions of this nature; and, indeed, we were *forcibly* reminded in this respect of the *inimitable* entertainment of three years ago." If a speaker indulges in this style of oratory, it is only considerate on the part of the reporter to tone it down by the omission of some of the superlatives. All speakers, it is true, will not approve of the operation. The late Hugh Stowell, of Liverpool, was greatly given to exaggeration of this kind. I once reported a speech of his in which, as a *verbatim* report was required, I preserved all his adjectives. I knew that he would revise the report, and thought that he would probably strike out some of his favourite epithets. To my surprise he not only left them all in, but inserted a good many more!

These are but a few hints showing the direction in which the young journalist should work in order to acquire a clear and accurate style of writing. On this and on other departments of literary composition I would refer the student to one or two text-books, from which he may derive much useful assistance and many salutary warnings. Bain's Rhetoric and Composition (Longmans) is a well-known and valued authority. Part I. (3/6), dealing with the intellectual elements of style, will be found very serviceable, and may be read with advantage even by an experienced hand. "Longman's School Composition," by Mr. D. Salmon (2/6) and Dr. Abbott's "How to Write Clearly" (Seeley), are two popular school-books on the same subject, and may be accepted as trustworthy guides.

CHAPTER XXVIII.

THE ETHICS OF REPORTING.

HAVING dealt with the various departments of shorthand work and pretty fully described their chief features, I desire to say something on the ethics of shorthand employment, the moral considerations surrounding it, and the relations which should subsist (1) between Shorthand writers and their employers; (2) between Shorthand writers themselves; and (3) between Shorthand writers and the speakers whose words they are called upon to chronicle. All that I have to say on the subject will, I think, come under one or other of these three heads.

1. As to the relations between Shorthand writers and their employers, they are so varied in their character that it is difficult to describe them in a few words. It is of course safe to say that, as in all cases of employer and employed, there should be the strictest mutual confidence and a desire to promote each other's interests. In the case of the Shorthand clerk or amanuensis, who is paid a regular salary, there is the same relation between him and his principal as there is in the case of any other clerical assistant, except perhaps that in some instances it is of a more confidential character. The assistant who has been for years engaged in taking down and transcribing the correspondence of his employer, becomes the repository of a great deal of information with regard not only to his business affairs but to his private history, and occupies a position of trust which can only be properly filled by a person of high honour and integrity. It is hardly necessary to say that any information thus acquired should never be revealed to others. No greater breach of trust could be committed than the making known elsewhere of what has been dictated in the office or in the study. The Shorthand writer usually keeps his own note books, and they should never be allowed to go into the hands of others who might make an improper use of them. I have known one or two instances in which

unprincipled amanuenses have sought to make capital of notes which have been dictated to them in the strictest confidence. In one case the notes related to some contemplated legal proceedings, and they were actually offered—for a consideration—to the persons against whom the proceedings were to be directed. It is scarcely possible to conceive of a more shameless and disgraceful violation of trust. I am glad to think that such occurrences are very exceptional. No business could be properly conducted if its employés were thus unmindful of their allegiance.

The case of the newspaper reporter is different. Nearly all his notetaking is for the express purpose of publication to the world. He may, therefore, be said to have a certain duty to the public for whom he is catering, but he is primarily responsible to his employer, the proprietor or editor of his newspaper, whose lawful instructions he is bound to follow. I say "lawful," because it is just possible that he may be required to do his work unfairly and dishonourably, and no reporter or other employé is under any such obligation. If he is instructed to give special prominence to certain speakers, or to certain parts of their speeches, I think he should scrupulously follow his instructions, even though he may think them unwise. or even to a certain extent unfair to other speakers whom he may regard as possessing superior claims. The responsibility of selection in such cases is not his own, and he may reasonably shelter himself behind his chief, and plead his instructions in extenuation of any want of judgment or fairness. But if he is expected to report in such a way as to give a false impression of a speech, to omit some vital point which is essential to the apprehension of the rest, or by some artful gloss to expose the speaker to ridicule or condemnation, no such shelter or plea should avail him. However briefly he may be required to report, he should insist upon reporting accurately. Happily, there are very few cases in which he is expected to do otherwise. It is to the interest of a newspaper proprietor to give his readers accurate reports, and he looks to his reporters to supply that commodity. But I have known instances in which requests have been made of the nature I have indicated. No honourable reporter, however, should allow himself to be the instrument of personal or political animosity. If he has a duty to his employer, he has also, as we shall see, a duty to the speaker, and he has no right to be a party to anything in the nature of misrepresentation. Subject to this he is, as I have said, bound to act upon his instructions, even though he may be acting in opposition to his own judgment. It may be at times difficult to draw the line, and to say how far he should go in the required direction, but in these cases he must be guided by his own sense of what is just to himself as well as to others.

I suppose there are few newspaper reporters of long experience who have not at times been tempted by pecuniary considerations to depart from the strict line of duty towards the journals which they represent. One of the commonest forms of bribery of this class is that of "keeping things out of the paper." A man appears before a police court, and is extremely solicitous that his name should not be paraded in the daily broad sheet. A guinea offered to the reporter may secure his object, and if the reporter is not scrupulous, the public hears nothing of the matter. Those who have accepted this kind of "hush money" have sometimes sought to justify it by saying that no one is injured. It is a poor excuse for neglect of duty. Possibly the case was of no great public importance, and no injury was done to the paper by not reporting it. If so, well and good. But no high-minded reporter will consent to receive a bribe for such an omission. If he withholds the report, it should be on wholly different considerations, and he should not run the risk of having his judgment warped by a pecuniary recompense.

Another form of bribery is that of inducing a reporter to aid a business concern, an exhibition, or a movement of any kind, by "writing it up." It is so easy to write a laudatory paragraph; and, after all, everyone knows what value to attach to newspaper effusions of that kind. That is the excuse sometimes offered for indiscriminate or undeserved eulogy, and for the acceptance of an honorarium for penning it. But, surely, it is not consistent with a high sense of honour and responsibility; and if the Press is to maintain a high tone and merit the confidence of the public, its contributors must be above yielding to temptations of this description.

But what is to be said when a grateful speaker, who finds

himself well and fully reported, sends a douceur, in money or in kind, to the reporter who has faithfully recorded his words? Such a recognition is not altogether unknown. It is not a bribe, but an acknowledgment of services rendered. Each reporter must decide for himself whether he should receive such a gift or not. I know that in some instances it has been politely declined, while in others it has been thankfully accepted. Everything depends upon the manner in which it is offered, and the relationship existing between the parties. If it is open to the suspicion of patronage, or of a payment for future favours, it should be declined without the slightest hesitation. This, however, is a matter which more properly belongs to the last of the three heads which I have mentioned, and I dismiss it without further remark.

The employment of the professional shorthand writer differs, as we have seen, from that of the reporter. He is not a salaried servant, but is employed for special work on special occasions, receiving his professional fees like a lawyer, or a doctor, or an artist; but his obligations to his principals, or "clients," though temporary, are none the less binding so long as they last. He is bound to do his best to carry out his instructions, and to guard faithfully any confidential information which he may acquire in the course of his work. A great deal of his employment is in the Law Courts, which are open to the public, and as to this, no seal of silence can be imposed upon him; but there are times when his assistance is required at meetings of a strictly private character, to which he is only admitted by virtue of his professional engagement, and on all such occasions his mouth should be closed as to anything that has transpired which is not intended or desired to be made public. I mention this because it occasionally happens that a shorthand writer or reporter, who is connected with a public journal, may be called upon to take a private report of a meeting, say of the shareholders of a company, to which reporters of the Press are not admitted. His newspaper might be glad of the opportunity of publishing a report of the proceedings, but it can only do so if its own representative is permitted to be present. It is obvious that in such cases it would be a breach of confidence on the part of a reporter, who was engaged in his private capacity, to use his notes for any other purpose than that contemplated. If other reporters are admitted, or if he knows that there is no objection to his supplying a newspaper report, as well as a verbatim report for those who employ him, no blame can attach to him for doing so. But he should clearly recognise the distinction I have pointed out, and act accordingly.

A point of some delicacy occasionally arises in reference to note-taking in Court. If a Shorthand writer has received instructions to take notes of a case for a client, he may be asked to supply a transcript to another from whom no such instructions have been received. Is he at liberty to do so? It is frequently done, and no objection is offered. The proceedings are public, and it is open to anyone to report them; it may therefore be contended that the shorthand notes are not in any way privileged. But the original employer may say that the notes would not have been taken but for his instructions, and that he is entitled to their exclusive use. I cannot say that the practice on the subject is definitely settled. Some solicitors, however, expressly prohibit the notes they have ordered being transcribed for anyone but themselves, and where such a prohibition is made, it is usually attended to. If, however, a Shorthand writer, or a Shorthand writing firm, wishes to be in a position to supply transcripts to other persons than the first employer, there is nothing to prevent them from having a duplicate note taken, which can be used for the purpose. But this does not apply to proceedings of a private character, the notes of which should be held sacred, and no transcript should be made, without permission, for any but the original employer. If a subpœna is served upon a reporter, requiring him to produce his notes in Court, he is absolved from all responsibility in the matter; but he may, if desired, plead that his notes are privileged, and decline to produce them, in which case the Court itself will decide whether the circumstances are such as to entitle him to adopt that course.

A question has sometimes been raised as to the custody of shorthand notes. Shorthand writers have been requested, as has happened more than once in my own experience, to deliver up their notes to those on whose behalf they have been taken, the request being usually made with a view of ensuring that the notes shall not get into other hands. The demand is most unusual, and should not be complied with except under very special circumstances. It is the custom for a Shorthand writer to keep his own notes, and he may reasonably decline to give them up. They are taken in his own book, and are as much his property as a negative is the property of the photographer who takes it. He may not be able to use them without permission, but that is no reason why he should hand them over to another. It often happens, indeed, that the notes are taken in books containing other notes, and on the backs of the same leaves, so that it is impossible to separate them. But if the Shorthand writer agrees beforehand to send in his notes with his transcript, he is, of course, bound by the agreement.

2. Little need be said on the subject of the relations which should exist between Shorthand writers themselves. Working as they frequently do in collaboration, every effort should be made by them to promote harmony and good will. In the first place, every member of a corps should be ready and willing to do his full share of work. He should, if there is a time table, be in his seat and ready to begin his note-taking to the minute, not to say to the second. It may seem a trifling matter to be a minute or two late, but a minute or two out of a quarter of an hour's turn is a considerable percentage, and may mean a difference of five or ten minutes in transcribing. No one cares to work with a colleague who thus shirks his duty, and cannot be depended upon to be at his post at the appointed time. Again, the reporter or Shorthand writer should be not only punctual and diligent, but should be good tempered and genial in his intercourse with his confrères, and ready to lend them a helping hand in circumstances of trouble or difficulty. Where these qualities are absent, there is little chance of pleasant and harmonious working. Many opportunities are presented for their exercise, and much of the pleasantness of a reporter's occupation depends upon these continual interchanges of courtesy and mutual assistance.

And these agreeable relations should not only exist between colleagues belonging to the same staff, but between reporters engaged in connection with different and perhaps rival establishments. Meeting as they constantly do at the same table, and employed in recording the same proceedings, they may greatly assist each other in many ways. It is only a churlish reporter who will get a document or a manuscript from a speaker, and refuse to allow his brethren to look at it or copy it. There may be exceptional circumstances, in which he may be unable to comply with their request, but in ordinary cases there should be a willingness to extend, as widely as possible among the reporters present, whatever advantages can be obtained in this way. Some reporters have earned a deserved popularity for their considerate treatment of their fellow workers in matters of this kind, while others have only acquired a reputation for churlishness and ill-nature. In regard to note-taking, it is usual for reporters to refer to their notes to verify any passage as to which a brother scribe may be in doubt. Especially should an older or more experienced hand be willing to render assistance of this character to his younger or less skilled brethren. He may not always be able to read over an entire speech, nor perhaps should he be required to do so, but he should at least be willing to refer to any doubtful or difficult passages, and generally to give such help as he may himself be glad at times to receive from others. It is no doubt rather trying for an accomplished hand to be asked to supply wholesale omissions for the benefit of an inefficient reporter, but here, as in so many other matters, it is better to err on the side of considerateness and generosity than on the side of illiberality and discourtesy.

3. The relationship of reporters to speakers is one of a peculiar character. It is not the relation of employer and employed, and yet there is a distinct obligation on the part of the reporter to act fairly towards the persons whose speeches he reports. Not that he is obliged to report them fully, but that what he does report shall represent, as far as space will permit, the meaning intended to be conveyed. No speaker has a right to complain that he is briefly reported. He has no claim to the space allotted to him in the newspaper. His speeches are reported, not to oblige him, but for the information of the public. He has, however, the right to require that he shall not be misrepresented, and that, at any rate, the general purport of what he says shall be fairly presented to the reader. Some speakers have declared that they would rather not be reported at all, than have their speeches passed through the condensing apparatus of the reporter's brain and pen. That

may be their individual feeling, but they can hardly expect to have effect given to it.

In regard to questions of style, and the extent to which the reporter should be expected to correct slips of the tongue or errors in composition, I have perhaps said enough in the preceding pages. Few speakers are so accurate as not to require some slight amendment when their speeches come to be reported, and no one should consider himself qualified for the office of reporter who cannot supply the necessary emendations. I do not say that he should seek to transform an ill-arranged and badly-expressed speech into a well-written essay, such as the speaker might have penned if he had been at his desk instead of upon the platform. All that can reasonably be required of him is that he should correct grammatical slips, omit needless repetitions, and make the sentences read with some degree of smoothness. Anything beyond this, hardly comes within the province of the reporter. Nor is it always an easy task, especially in the case of a careless speaker. It is certainly a work for which the majority of speakers are anything but grateful. They have little idea of the trouble involved in the re-arrangement of their words and sentences. They read, perhaps, a report of their utterances, and too often take credit to themselves for what, in part at least, has been the work of the reporter. Herein, indeed, lies a great deal of the reporter's art, so to alter the language that he records as that the alteration shall hardly be perceptible to the speaker himself, so carefully have the characteristic features of his style been retained.

CHAPTER XXIX.

PHONOGRAPHY AND PRONUNCIATION.

ONE of the outward and audible signs of a good education is a careful and accurate pronunciation. One occasionally hears a well educated man drop his *h's* and otherwise mispronounce his words; but such cases are very exceptional. The practice of Shorthand should help to correct any tendency in that direction, and that for two reasons. In the first place, the reporter or Shorthand writer has frequent opportunities of listening to the best speakers; and in the second place, the phonetic character of his system (especially if he writes Phonography) directs his attention to the *sounds* of words more definitely and distinctly than the common longhand. He has therefore little excuse for orthoëpic inaccuracies. The advantage, however, of Phonography in the matter of pronunciation, is chiefly observable when the words are fully vocalized. In reading a phonographic letter, for example, one often notices some peculiarity of pronunciation clearly indicated, to which the common spelling would afford no clue. I have seen the word *Tuesday* written  showing clearly enough that the writer was in the habit of pronouncing the word with a  *ch* at the commencement. In the case of the word *leisure*, the vowel used by the writer will show whether he says  or ; and so the use of the vowel in *neither* will be proof positive as to whether the writer says 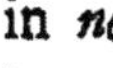 or 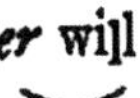

I do not of course say that every difference in pronunciation can be marked by Phonography. There are minute variations which it would be impossible to express in a practical system intended for every-day use. There are many dialectical peculiarities, especially in the pronunciation of the single vowels and diphthongs, which are mere shades, *nuances* as the French call them, which sometimes require a trained ear to detect, and which it would be idle to attempt to reproduce in a popular system of writing, although they might be indicated by a very much enlarged alphabet for the purpose of minute and scientific analysis. The first long vowel, for example, in the phonographic alphabet, *ah*, is pronounced in the West of England with a less broad sound, very much resembling, if it is not identical with, the sound of the second long vowel before an *r*, as in *mare*, *care*, which is broader than when the same vowel precedes any other consonant, as *make*, *cape*. There are also differences in the pronunciation of the first short vowel, as in *man*, *hat*, words which in the North of England are often pronounced more broadly, the vowel having very much the Continental sound of the letter *a*. In some parts of Scotland the long *eh* (ā) is pronounced as a closer vowel than in England, and it is not always easy to distinguish, except from the context, whether a Scotchman says  or  for *great*. So the vowel in *day* is made almost as close as that in *Dee*. It is true that the same speakers are also in the habit of pronouncing the long *ē* closer than is usual with Englishmen, so that there is, perhaps, an equal interval between the two vowels *eh* and *ē*. Thus *deer* would be pronounced like the French *dire*, in which the vowel is much finer and closer than in the English word, though many Englishmen fail to perceive the difference. There is also another variety of the long *ā*. Most English speakers make it almost a double vowel, the last element being a very short *e*, resembling indeed the common dissyllabic diphthong *eh-i* as in *clayey;* while others (especially I think in Yorkshire) insist on making it a pure single vowel. One says  *pay*, using the pure single vowel, and another  with the last element, the *e*, more or less distinctly pronounced. Some persons profess to make a distinction between such words as *gait* and *gate*, *pain* and *pane*, giving the double sound in the one case and the single in the other; but I do not think this is the general practice among good speakers. Again, the vowel *au*, represented in Phonography by the first long dash, is often pronounced as a double vowel, the last element being what is known as the indistinct vowel *uh*, so that we get the intensely disagreeable, not to say vulgar, combination *au-uh*. When I was in the habit of teaching phonographic classes I constantly noticed that in repeating the vowels together, many pupils persisted in saying, *ah*, *ā*, *ee*, *au-uh*, *ō*, *ōō*. I invariably pointed out the error, and made the class go through the sounds again and again till they pronounced them accurately.

With regard to the diphthongs ᵛ *i* and ʌ *ow*, there are great differences in pronunciation. The Cockney makes the first element a broad *ah*, and says *mah-in* for *mine*; and a similar pronunciation, but perhaps a little broader, may be observed in the northern counties. The best speakers make the first element of the diphthong much more close; and some go to the other extreme and make it so close as to appear affected or "finiking." It is not easy to say what is the precise analysis of this vowel as uttered by the best speakers. There is no question that the last element is *e*; but whether the first is *ĕ*, *ă*, *ŭ*, or the indistinct vowel, is a debateable point. It seems to elude detection. Perhaps the phonograph, when worked very slowly, may help to elucidate the matter.

The Londoner also broadens considerably the first element of the diphthong *ow*, and makes it *ah-oo* or *ă-oo*, which is very objectionable to a sensitive ear.

The diphthong ₙ *u* is also the subject of some variations in sound. In Wales, and I think in some parts of the eastern counties, one hears it pronounced as two distinct vowels, *e-oo*, instead of *yoo*. The *y* is usually pronounced as a consonant or nearly so. Some profess to make a distinction between the first sound in *useful* and *youthful*. They are, in fact, identical; and to say "an useful thing" is as cacophonic as to say "an youthful person."

With regard to the consonants, there is comparatively little variation. With one exception, they are sounded alike in all parts of the country. That exception is the letter *r*, which is the subject of several very distinct varieties. Londoners are very fond of dropping it altogether when it ends a syllable or a word, or is followed by another consonant, making no difference between *father* and *farther*, *alms* and *arms*, but slightly trilling the letter when it begins a word or syllable. In Scotland the soft English *r* is scarcely known, and the letter is trilled wherever it occurs; and in Northumberland and Durham it is represented by what is known as the burr, a somewhat guttural sound, like the *r* grasséyé of the French. It is produced, I believe, by a vibration of the uvula against the root of the tongue. In the West of England again the letter has a very peculiar sound, which it is difficult for a stranger to the western counties to reproduce. It is as characteristic of Somersetshire and Devonshire as is the long *āā* to which I have alluded; it being rarely heard in any other part of the country.

One peculiarity of the letter *r* is, that it slightly modifies some of the vowels that precede it, especially *ā* and *ō*, which are somewhat broadened in sound when in this position, as in *mare*, *Mary*, *store*, *story*, where the vowel is distinctly broader than in the words *may*, *stow*. The letter *r* also has a tendency to convert a short vowel preceding it into a kind of indistinct vowel, which it is not easy to identify. The vowel in *mercy* is very different from that in *met*, and the word is usually pronounced by Englishmen more like *murcy*, though Scotchmen very nearly preserve the *ĕ* sound. Phonography once had a special sign to represent this indistinct vowel. It was called *uh*, and was written with the second-place dash parallel to the consonant. Mr Pitman, however, after three years' practice with this additional vowel, thought it wise to discard it and to use one of the short vowels in its place, although it involves a slight departure from the sound actually uttered.

These and other variations that I might mention, are not such as a phonographer distinguishes in his ordinary writing. Of course, it would be easy to multiply the written signs to such an extent as would enable the writer to express the different shades of sound to which I have referred, but, as I have said, it is not every ear that can detect these subtle distinctions, and for practical purposes it is found best to disregard them in writing.

There are, however, other varieties of pronunciation which can easily be preserved, and it is to these that I wish to draw special attention, because, as I have already said, I do not think that full advantage is taken of the use which Phonography might be made to subserve in this respect. There is a good deal of inaccurate pronunciation, even among fairly well educated people, which the ordinary spelling does not in any way serve to correct, but which a phonographic student is able easily to rectify. There are, of course, many words as to the pronunciation of which authorities differ, and neither can be said to be absolutely incorrect. I have already referred to and The word *gaseous* has three or four modes of pronunciation, ; and I cannot say which is the most correct, that is, which is most commonly used by educated persons ; that being, I suppose, the only standard of accuracy. *Isolate* has two pronunciations, which is perhaps the most common, and One man says *Celtic* and *pharmaceutical*, and another says and One says *myth* and another *Issue* is pronounced both and ; *chivalry* both and ; and no one can say that either of these pronunciations is wrong, each having authority or custom on its side. But this is not the class of words with which I am now dealing. All that I need say respecting them is, that the common spelling is no guide as to the pronunciation of the writer, but that if all wrote phonetically, or if books were so printed (as, of course, in due time they will be) the reader would be at no loss in the matter, but would have the satisfaction of knowing not only what the writer had written, but how he would give it vocal utterance. I am rather referring to the decidedly and admittedly inaccurate pronunciations into which tolerably educated people sometimes fall, but which are extremely common among the imperfectly educated, and which no amount of mere book reading will enable them to rectify. A man may go on saying *put* all his life, and may be a most industrious reader without suspecting for a moment that he has been mispronouncing the word, there being nothing in the spelling to set him right. Many persons persist in saying *infinite*—I have often heard clergymen and singers so pronounce it—and they can appeal to the spelling for confirmation. One sometimes hears even classical scholars say *diphthong*, and *diphtheria*, instead of , and Here, it is true, even the common spelling might set them right; but then the common spelling is such an untrustworthy guide in matters of pronunciation, that it is not surprising that it should be disregarded. Speaking of *ph*, I am reminded that in some parts of England, particularly in Norfolk and Suffolk, the word *nephew* is pronounced instead of ; the orthography being followed rather than the general custom. It is no uncommon thing to hear persons speaking of the *zoological* gardens. Here again it is the spelling that misleads. I once heard a man speak of the *Cooperative* stores, misguided in the same way by the *oo*, which has usually the sound of *England* is by some persons pronounced instead of , following the spelling and not the established usage. So with *knowledge* and *acknowledge*, which are sometimes pronounced according to a somewhat archaic style and , instead of and ; the orthography again being responsible for what we must now call an orthoëpic error. To the same cause may be attributed the fact that some persons insist on saying *clerk* instead of And those who, using the words *epitome* and *extempore*, call them and , instead of and can urge the common spelling in extenuation of their fault.

One of the most common errors of pronunciation with imperfectly educated people, and even with well-informed persons who have not lost their provincialisms, is the misuse and interchange of the two short vowels and as in *but* and *foot*. I have already referred to the mispronunciation for *put*, to which may be added *full* instead of ; *stood* instead of The curious thing about these words is, that the man who says for is very likely to say *but* instead of , and perhaps will go back to the second place vowel in *butcher* and call it These mistakes are chiefly observable in the Midland and Northern counties. As an illustration, I may mention that at a recent teachers' examination in the North, where there were twelve candidates, seven wrote the word , and four wrote the word correctly , another candidate (perhaps being a little uncertain about the matter) artfully omitted the vowel.

Another frequent error may be noticed in connection with the last consonant in the phonetic alphabet, *ng*, which is (in the Midland counties especially, and in some parts of Lancashire) sometimes pronounced as a double consonant, namely, It is difficult to persuade such persons that there is no sound of *g* at the end of the words *sing, bring.* They will say *sing* and *singing,* *bring* and *bringing.* If they are phonographers it is possible that they may not *write* the words thus, notwithstanding they say it. They do not perceive the difference between *singer* and *linger;* *longer* (one who longs) and *longer* (more long); between *hanger* and *anger.*

I might cite many other instances of words of this class, in which the spelling renders no assistance to the student who wishes to acquire an accurate pronunciation; or, even worse, absolutely leads him astray. But these illustrations will perhaps suffice. What I wish to point out is, that phonographers who are in the habit of reading phonetic literature, have no excuse for not correcting any errors of this kind into which they may have fallen. The shorthand student who meets with the word *foot* and pronounces it is simply misreading his characters. It would seem impossible that a person could meet with the word *move* and pronounce it , but I have heard it done; just as I have heard the word *discover,* pronounced , notwithstanding the use of the vowel

I have called attention to these things, not only from my experience in past years as a teacher, but still more from some recent experience that I have had in connection with the examination of teachers. It is not, perhaps, surprising that young phonographers should at first fail to perceive the full phonetic significance of the shorthand words they meet with in reading; but I confess to a feeling of astonishment that teachers themselves in some parts of the country, notwithstanding their phonetic experience, have not discarded some of their provincialisms, and other errors of pronunciation, which the very characters that they have been teaching to others should have brought to their notice as errors to be corrected. It should be one of the functions of a phonetic teacher to assist his pupils in the matter of accurate pronunciation. If he is himself at fault in this respect, it is a case of the blind leading the blind, or the deaf guiding the deaf. I know that many teachers regard this as a part of their duty, and are careful to point out mistakes of this class which their pupils may make, and to show how they may themselves correct them, if they will carefully notice the manner in which the shorthand words are built up. But this is by no means universally the case; and I venture respectfully to suggest that those teachers who have not taken this subject into consideration, should give heed to it in the future, in order that they and their pupils alike may reap the full advantage which Phonography, in this respect as in so many others, places within their reach.

I should like also to suggest to purveyors of phonetic literature, that they should do their best to preserve an accurate pronunciation of everything that they place before their readers. Errors under this head should be as carefully avoided as mis-spellings in the current orthography. It is not doing Phonography justice to use it as a vehicle for anything but the speech of educated men and women. That is the moral of the present chapter. I think also that phonographic teachers might do some good among their pupils by impressing upon them the necessity of *distinct articulation*. The slovenly, smudgy manner in which English is commonly spoken is a national disgrace. The subject is certainly connected with the science of phonetics and the art of Phonography; and, if the teacher will bear it in mind, he may, while giving his shorthand lessons, act in some degree as an instructor in elocution.

Perhaps I may be permitted to add a word or two on the use of Phonography as an aid to the pronunciation of foreign languages. This is sometimes perhaps exaggerated, but that is no reason why we should fail to form a just estimate of the advantages which phonetic shorthand offers in this respect. There are many minute details of pronunciation and intonation in connection with different languages which distinguish a native from a foreigner, but which cannot well be graphically expressed. This can only be learned by means of the living voice; and we all know how difficult it often is, even with this assistance, to catch the little delicate shades and peculiarities that distinguish one language from another. But these niceties apart, the student may find in Phonography a very convenient mode of recording the pronunciation of most of the widely spoken European languages. For this purpose a few additional symbols are needed for sounds that do not occur in English. The chief of these sounds are the French *u*, represented by the third dash written parallel to the consonant, *du;* the French *eu*, equivalent to the German *ö*, represented by the parallel dash in the first position, *feu*, *schön;* the French *e*, as in *le*, *de*, also heard at the end of the German words *habe*, *liebe*, etc., represented by the second place parallel dash *le*, *me*, *meine*), the guttural sounds of *k*, *g*, occurring in German and other languages, represented by ; the French nasals which can be represented either by (the English sound of this letter not occurring in French), with the required vowel preceding it, or by ; and French *l'mouillé*, represented by I say nothing about the Oriental languages with their aspirated consonants, or the African "clicks," or any of the more unusual sounds which the European can hardly be expected to imitate, even if his ear detects them. To represent these adequately, a very much enlarged alphabet would be required, which would be beyond the range of the practical work that we are now contemplating. With the few additional signs I have mentioned, a student of French, German, and other Continental languages, ought to have no difficulty in marking, at least with approximate accuracy, if not with extreme scientific precision, the pronunciation of the words he is learning—certainly with much greater accuracy than he is likely to attain by a reference to the familiar but often irritating pronouncing dictionary.

POSTSCRIPT.

I have not, as is said to be the custom with ladies in their correspondence, kept the most important part of my book for the postscript. There are, however, one or two topics, not altogether without interest, on which I desire to add a few words.

Since the foregoing pages were printed, the subject of an educational test for reporters has again come before the Institute of Journalists, at its annual meeting in Edinburgh. The recommendation of the committee to which the subject had been referred was fully discussed, and finally adopted. I have alluded to it elsewhere, and will only add to what has been already said that I am very glad that the members of the Institute have, by a large majority, given their sanction to the proposal. It has been remitted to the Council to carry it out, and press-men will await with interest, if not with anxiety, the steps taken to this end. It is hardly likely that any special examination will be instituted in the ordinary subjects of education, there being many excellent examining bodies open to the public whose diplomas would suffice for the purpose. The main duty of the Council will be to indicate the subjects in which they expect their candidates to pass, and the educational bodies whose diplomas they will accept. In regard to special and technical qualifications, of which a knowledge of Shorthand is one of the most important, no doubt it will be considered desirable to establish a special examination, and this will, of course, be designed to test not simply the candidate's expertness in verbatim note-taking, but also his ability to condense or summarise. The result of such examinations, general and professional, can hardly fail to raise the qualifications and improve the status of British journalists. They are now becoming a numerous and influential body, and it is only fitting that the entrance to their ranks, while not made unduly difficult, should be safe-guarded by some such test as the Institute has declared to be necessary. My own opinion is that the proposed examination need not be a very wide one, its main object being not to test how much a candidate knows on a great variety of subjects, but rather to obtain an indication of his general aptitude, his readiness of perception, and his ability to present his own thoughts, or the thoughts of others, in good grammatical English. I think that Latin (elementary), and French and German, should form part of the examination. As to English subjects, I should be willing, after specifying as compulsory one or two of the most important, to allow the candidates to make their own selection of the others.

I avail myself of the opportunity presented by my Postscript of supplying an omission or two with reference to newspaper reporting. The first relates to the subject of transcribing notes when travelling. Now that long reports are so often sent over the wire, the practice of transcribing notes *en route*, say in a railway train, is not so common as it was in the days when this method of transmission was unknown or but rarely adopted. But it is still an occasional necessity, and provision should be made for it. Except in the Pullman carriages, there are none of the ordinary facilities for writing, and the reporter who has to transcribe in the train should provide himself with a thin board or some other extemporised desk—the cover of a book will often suffice—on which to rest his slips, which may be secured by an india-rubber band. It is not convenient to write on the knee, in consequence of the joltings of the train. It is better to sit upright, holding the paper, &c., in the left hand, and not leaning against the back of the carriage. The position is not in itself the most comfortable; but it is the best for writing purposes. When it is known that the notes will have to be thus transcribed, the reporter may write the lines very widely apart, so as to be able to write the longhand transcript between them; or he may take the notes on the left-hand margin of the paper—about one-third of the whole, leaving the remaining two-thirds for the transcript. If the work has to be done during the night and in a badly-lighted carriage, some kind of reading lamp should be used, to avoid a strain on the eyes. A little electric lamp can now be obtained, costing about £2, the burner being attached to the coat button-hole in such a way as to throw the light very conveniently on the book or paper held in the hand. This, it need hardly be said, is a great comfort both to the reader and the writer.

The other omission has reference to the salaries commonly paid to newspaper reporters. These vary greatly, according to the nature of the services rendered and the position of the papers. Parliamentary reporters receive from three or four to six or seven guineas a week during the session, some of the older hands on the London papers being retained at the same salaries throughout the year On country papers the remuneration ranges from thirty shillings to five or six guineas a week; but, as shown elsewhere, there are in many cases, frequent opportunities of doing private shorthand work and thus securing an additional income. In the absence of any express stipulation, a month's notice is usually required on either side to terminate an engagement.